COMING TO AMERICA

COMING TO AMERICA

Immigrants from the BRITISH ISLES

SHIRLEY BLUMENTHAL
AND
JEROME S. OZER

DELACORTE PRESS / NEW YORK

Published by
Delacorte Press
1 Dag Hammarskjold Plaza
New York, N.Y. 10017

The poem "Inis Fál" from *Collected Poems* by James
Stephens is reprinted by permission of Macmillan Publishing Co., Inc., and by permission of Mrs. Iris Wise and
Macmillan, London and Basingstoke. Copyright 1918 by
Macmillan Publishing Co., Inc., renewed 1946 by James
Stephens.

Copyright © 1980 by Visual Education Corporation

Manufactured in the United States of America
First printing

Picture research by Anne Phalon

Designed by Rhea Braunstein

LIBRARY OF CONGRESS CATALOGING IN PUBLICATION DATA

Blumenthal, Shirley, 1943–
   Coming to America.

   Bibliography: p.
   Includes index.
   SUMMARY: Discusses those people who came to the
United States from the British Isles as the settlers of new
English colonies and, later, as immigrants seeking a home
in a new nation. Includes a chronology of the U. S.
immigration laws.
   1.   British Americans—History—Juvenile literature.
   2.   United States—Ethnic relations—Juvenile literature.
   [1.   British Americans—History.   2.   Ethnic relations.
   3.   United States—Emigration and immigration.]
   I.   Ozer, Jerome S., joint author.   II.   Title.
E184.B7B55   973'.042   80-65841
ISBN 0-440-01071-3

Contents

Illustrations appear after page 88

Introduction

Americans don't often think of the early immigrants from the British Isles as immigrants.

That may be because from the first, the English did not consider themselves alien. They saw themselves not as immigrants, but as colonists, taking possession of the land that the luck of exploration, and success in war and diplomacy, had made theirs. Because most of these immigrants had been discontent at home, they did not want to create a replica of England, but a new nation with values that were considered radical by the English who stayed at home.

By the middle of the eighteenth century British immigration to the Colonies no longer meant just immigration from England. Scots, Welsh, and Irish joined the swell from all corners of the British Isles. They were all British subjects, and English was their language, along with their native Gaelic and Welsh. They were, in fact, used to living in a culture dominated by English law and institutions. In the thirteen Colonies the ground rules were familiar. And for these immigrants, as for the English who had left home in despair of gaining the political, economic, or social rights they wanted, the Colonies offered both a refuge and an opportunity. With hard work, valiant fighting, and perseverance, the new immigrants joined the earlier colonists in the revolution against England. A turning point had come: The United States of America was born, and British subjects became citizens of the American republic.

Chapter 1

The First Ventures

Europeans began to look for a way to get to Asia by sailing west, rather than east around Africa, toward the end of the fifteenth century. The discovery of land that lay in the way was made by accident. Portuguese sailors had passed very close, but Cristoforo Colombo, a Genoese sailing under the flag of Spain, was the first to claim land for the crown of Spain on the island of San Salvador, in what is now the Bahamas, in 1492. Columbus, as he is known in English, undertook a second voyage in 1493 to colonize another island, which he named Española, today called Hispaniola. He insisted the lands he discovered were part of "the Indies," by which he meant the eastern extremities of Asia. Before he could start out on his third voyage, England found another coast of the New World.

King Henry VII of England had refused to back Columbus on his initial voyage, but in 1496 he granted authority to Giovanni Caboto, another

1

Genoa-born navigator (and countryman of Columbus), to discover lands as yet "unknown to all Christians."[1] John Cabot, as he is known in English, set sail in 1497, and after a voyage of about six weeks landed probably on Newfoundland and claimed it for King Henry. According to the royal records, Cabot's return voyage took only fifteen days. King Henry rewarded him for the acquisition of "the new isle," and Cabot set out again in 1498 to explore it further and to set up a trading colony. Like Columbus, Cabot thought this land was close to the East Indies. Cabot never returned from this voyage. After Cabot's disappearance, Polydore Vergil, an English historian, acidly commented that Cabot had

> found his new lands only in the ocean's bottom, to which he and his ship are thought to have sunk, since, after that voyage, he was never heard of more.[2]

Cabot had not found either gold or spices, as Columbus did, so the English were not impressed by his discoveries.

Afraid of the Spanish, who had already established colonies in America, and short of funds for further explorations, Henry VII did not pursue the discovery of the New World. His son, Henry VIII, became embroiled in the religious revolution known as the Reformation, which was sweeping across all of Europe in the sixteenth century. The Reformation in England brought about a break with the Church of Rome when Henry sought divorce from his wife and proclaimed a separate Church of England with himself at the head of it. Political as well as religious in nature, the Reformation left serious divisions between Catholics and Protestants that would last for centuries.

When Henry VIII's daughter Elizabeth took the throne in 1558, it became clear that England would be a Protestant country and the most powerful Protestant country in Europe. Queen Elizabeth I, with her merchants and adventurers, could begin to take possession of the North American lands that Cabot had claimed for England.

The Age of Elizabeth was a golden age for the English, and William Shakespeare summed up Elizabethan exuberance, pride, and self-confidence in his play *Richard II*, when John of Gaunt says:

> . . . this scepter'd isle,
> This earth of majesty, this seat of Mars,
> This other Eden, demi-paradise, . . .
> This happy breed of men, this little world,
> This precious stone set in silver sea, . . .
> This blessed plot, this earth, this realm,
>   this England.
>   (Act II, Scene 1)

England defeated the Spanish Armada in 1588 and became a great sea power, chartering many trade companies and opening sea routes. Commerce flourished, and merchants thrived. England became more prosperous, and living conditions for much of the population improved. But there was a darker side to Elizabethan life, expressed in the traditional nursery rhyme:

Hark, hark, the dogs do bark.
The beggars are coming to town.

While the new merchants and manufacturers were growing wealthy, thousands of peasants were driven to poverty. England's emerging woolen industry required land to graze sheep. The enclosure acts had been turning open farmlands into pasture land, and forcing tenant farmers off the land. Few tenants who still had land could pay the increasingly high rents. The result was a class of beggars and vagabonds, forced off the land and unable to find employment, who wandered the country trying to stay alive. A contemporary writer realized the seriousness of the situation and suggested emigration as a solution:

Our land [is] abounding with swarms of idle persons which having no means to relieve their misery, do likewise swarm in lewd and naughty practices. So that if we seek not some ways for their foreign employment, we must provide shortly more prisons and corrections for their bad conditions. It . . . is most profitable for our state to rid our multitudes of such as lie at home, pestering the land with pestilence and penury, and infecting one another with vice and villainy.[3]

So both merchant and beggar found the idea of going to America attractive. In addition, the relations between Protestant England and Catholic Spain had deteriorated into a permanent state of hostility. It seemed wise for England to counter Spain's colonial assets by establishing her own. Colonies would attract commercial interests by supplying raw materials and by being markets for the goods England would manufacture.

Richard Hakluyt was one of England's foremost propagandists for expansion. In 1584 he wrote *A Discourse Concerning Western Planting* to persuade the queen to back Sir Walter Raleigh's proposal to establish a colony in North America. To Elizabethans, the word "planting" meant settlement or colonization. Hakluyt put forward a number of arguments:

> That this western discovery will be greatly for the enlargement of the gospel of Christ, whereunto the princes of the reformed religion are chiefly bound. . . .
> That this enterprise will be for the manifold employment of numbers of idle men. . . .
> That this voyage will be a great bridle to the Indies [that belong to] the King of Spain. . . .
> That . . . the Indian treasure . . . [will come] to the Queen's most excellent majesty. . . .
> That hereby the revenues . . . of her Majesty shall mightily be enlarged. . . .
> That speedy planting in diverse fit places is

most necessary upon these lucky western discoveries, for fear of the danger of being prevented by other nations which have the like intentions. . . .
That by these colonies the Northwest passage to Cathay and China may easily, quickly, and perfectly be searched out. . . .
That the Queen of England's title to all the west . . . from Florida to the Arctic Circle is more lawful and right than the Spaniard's or any other Christian prince's.[4]

Hakluyt argued well, for in April 1584 the queen gave Raleigh the authority and money to send out an expedition to America. One of Raleigh's captains wrote an enthusiastic account of arriving with two vessels near Roanoke, reporting the country "so delightful and desirable," with a variety of good fruits, trees, game, and fowl "in such plenty and variety that no epicure could desire more than this New World did seem naturally to afford." The native Indians were "so innocent and ignorant of politics, tricks, and cunning, and so desirous of the company of the English" that they did not seem "likely to oppose the settling of the English near them. Her Majesty . . . [was] so well pleased . . . that as the greatest mark of honor she could do the discovery, she called the country by the name of Virginia,"[5] after herself (she was known as "the Virgin Queen").

The next April Raleigh sent out one hundred men

to set up a trading colony in Virginia, which covered most of what is now the east coast of the United States. The native Americans, or "Indians," in fact resented the English, and they argued over the food they would supply to the colonists. Though a few Englishmen were impressed by the native American chiefs and the structure of tribal life, most felt superior to the Indians. They felt they had a right to take the land as theirs without negotiating or establishing friendly relations with the Indians. Within a year there were several killings of Indians and Englishmen. In June 1586, when Sir Francis Drake's fleet, fresh from raids on Spanish settlements in the West Indies, stopped at Roanoke Island (in what is now North Carolina), the unhappy colonists boarded his ships to return to England.

A second "planting" expedition set out in May 1587 to establish a permanent colony, the "city of Raleigh," with 117 men, women, and children. Most of them were English, but a few were Irish. They landed at Roanoke Island, where they faced continuing hostility from the native Americans. It was in this city of Raleigh that Virginia Dare was born —the first English child to be born in North America.

Three years later Raleigh sent ships with supplies to the colony. The place was deserted. The only clue to the colonists' fate was the word CROATOAN carved on a tree. Croatoan was the name of a nearby island, but storms prevented the fleet from sailing there, and it returned to England. Nothing more was ever learned about the demise of the city of Raleigh and the fate of the first British immigrants and little Virginia Dare.

The next group of British immigrants to "plant" in the world arrived in 1607 at Jamestown in Virginia, then at Plymouth in the north in 1620. For the rest of the seventeenth century, the immigrants from Britain were mainly English, and their colonies prospered.

Chapter 2

The People of the British Isles

In later centuries the Scots, Irish, and Welsh peoples joined the English in coming to America. They all had similar reasons for leaving the British Isles: to look for economic opportunity, social mobility, and political and religious liberty. But the reasons for the emigration of the Scots, Irish, and Welsh were complicated by the fact that, for the most part, they considered themselves subject peoples dominated by foreign rule: English rule.

During ancient and medieval times peoples from continental Europe—Celts, Romans, Saxons, Angles, Jutes, Danes, and Norwegians—had come to the British islands. Some came as settlers and traders; most came as invaders and conquerors. The English, Welsh, Scots, and Irish developed out of this amalgam, each group in its unique way, with its own culture and language.

The islands were made up of many small kingdoms. The first of the British peoples to unite their kingdoms into the beginnings of a nation were the English. When the last conqueror from abroad, William of Normandy, invaded England in 1066, he had but to defeat one king and one army to make himself master of the realm.

Even before the Norman Conquest, the English had tried to make their power felt among their Scottish and Welsh neighbors. Many of their military efforts were to prevent raids on English fields and villages and to establish clear borders. But these compaigns also aimed to impose English influence over other princes and kings. William of Normandy and his successors on the English throne carried both these trends to completion. They unified England under strong central rule and brought neighboring peoples under English domination.

The first to succumb were the Welsh, who inhabited a small, mountainous peninsula on the west coast of Britain. The Welsh kings, though lords of their own domains, had been forced to show homage and pay tribute monies to the English throne since 973, in effect, recognizing the English king as an overlord. But in 1272 the most powerful of the Welsh princes, Llewelyn ab Gruffydd, refused to carry out these duties. As a result King Edward I of England invaded Wales and over the next twenty years crushed Welsh resistance. The Welsh became English subjects, ruled by the English crown and governed by English law. To symbolize English authority, Edward gave his son the title Prince of Wales in 1301. This has ever since been the title of the heir to the English throne.

Welsh nationalism did not die with Edward's conquest. There were occasional flare-ups against taxation or mandatory military service. A large-scale Welsh revolt in 1400 took the English ten years to put down. But the Welsh had neither the political unity nor the resources to counter the much greater might of England. Finally, Wales ceased to be a separate entity after Henry VIII broke with the Catholic Church. Determined to unify his realm, he passed an act of union through Parliament in 1536 annexing Wales to England.

As they did with the Welsh, the English kings also tried to extort homage and tribute from the Scots. Some English kings had more success than others, but finally, the armies of William the Conqueror and his son William II subdued the Scots completely. There followed two centuries of relative peace. The Scots of the Lowlands—the rolling hills and plains closest to England—began to copy English speech and learn English ways. But the people of the Highlands—the northern mountainous region—remained for many centuries true to ancient tribal traditions. The Highlanders' language remained Gaelic, their dress the tartan cape, their social organization the clan, and their loyalties to the clan chiefs.

Edward I, the conqueror of Wales, interfered in the affairs of Scotland and claimed his right as overlord. He punished Scottish resistance from the forces of John Balliot by launching a devastating invasion in 1296, during which he appropriated the Stone of Destiny from the Abbey of Scone. The Stone of

Scone had been the traditional coronation seat of Scotland's kings. Edward had it removed to Westminster Abbey, where it was installed at the base of England's coronation throne.

Edward's aggressions touched off 250 years of more or less continuous warfare between England and Scotland. The Scots regarded these as wars of independence; the English regarded them as rebellion and treason. A "declaration of independence" written by Scottish barons in 1320 expressed the Scots' continuing defiance of England.

> So long as a hundred of us remain alive we will never be subject to the English king. It is not for glory, riches or honors that we fight, but for liberty alone, which no worthy man will lay down, save with his life.[1]

In 1502 King James IV of Scotland wanted to end the ages of war between his land and England. He negotiated a treaty of "perpetual peace," one of a long line of such treaties (perpetual peace between England and Scotland tended to be short-lived).

James then married Margaret Tudor, the daughter of King Henry VII of England and sister of Henry VIII. The granddaughter of James and Margaret, Mary Stuart, came of age to assume the crown of Scotland in 1559. She also revived the hopes of Catholics, who wished to reclaim the throne of England. The Catholic Church considered Queen Elizabeth of England (Mary Stuart's cousin) an illegitimate ruler, because the Church did not recognize the marriage of divorced Henry VIII to

Anne Boleyn, Elizabeth's mother. Also, Elizabeth was Europe's most vigorous royal champion of Protestantism.

Catholics acclaimed Mary Stuart the lawful queen of England by virtue of her legitimate descent from Henry VII. When Mary tried to get help from European Catholics to back her claim, Scottish Protestant forces rose against her, and she fled to England. Elizabeth kept her cousin imprisoned in relative comfort for twenty years. Finally, to protect her throne from conspiracies to place Mary upon it, Elizabeth had the Queen of Scots beheaded for her part in encouraging such conspiracies.

Elizabeth, "the Virgin Queen," died childless, however, and so the heir to the throne became Mary Stuart's son, James VI of Scotland, who had been raised by his Scottish guardians as a Puritan Protestant. He became James I of England in 1603. From that time on, the crowns of the two nations were united in one monarch. James I moved away from Puritanism, a faith that had many followers in Scotland and England, and, for political reasons, tried to impose the practices of the English Episcopal Church upon the Scots.

These policies were continued by James's son, Charles I. But Charles's high-handed ways proved to be his undoing. In 1641 the Parliament in London had a Puritan majority, and it challenged the king's authority in the name of religious and civil liberties. England plunged into a decade of civil war. At first, Scotland supported Parliament in the conflict. Then the Parliament forces under the leadership of Oliver

Cromwell executed Charles. Offended by regicide, the Scots remained royalist, backing Charles's son, also named Charles.

Cromwell's armies defeated the Scots, and English troops occupied the Lowlands. What little had remained of Scottish independence was lost, for the Scottish parliament was dissolved. In its place Scotland was allowed to send some representatives to the Parliament in London, from where all laws would come.

In 1660, two years after Cromwell's death, the Stuart monarchy was restored in the person of Charles II, son of Charles I. During his reign there were further struggles between the Puritan (Presbyterian) Scots and the Episcopal English. But Scots and English united to oppose Charles's Catholic brother, James II, who succeeded him. James abdicated in favor of his Protestant daughter, Mary, and her husband, William of Orange (a Dutch royal house) in the "Glorious," or Bloodless, Revolution. In 1707, under Queen Anne, William and Mary's daughter, Scotland, England, and Wales were united by the Act of Union. This act formed the Kingdom of Great Britain with a single ruler and a single parliament in London.

Scottish resistance flared up briefly in 1715 and more vigorously again in 1745–1746. There were still some Scots who supported the cause of the deposed Stuart king, James II. Although James was long dead, a grandson, yet another Charles ("Bonnie Prince Charlie"), still claimed that the throne of England was rightfully his, because he was the son of James's son, and the male line of descent always took precedence in such matters. Charles went to Scotland in 1745 from exile in France to press his claim, and many Highlanders joined in his cause.

The Highlanders had never been much assimilated into the Anglo-Scottish culture that had evolved in the Lowlands. They remained hunters and fishers, while the Lowlanders had become farmers and merchants. Loyalty was the cement of the Highland clans, and it was to their ideals of loyalty, honor, and independence from outside rule that Charles appealed. But the outnumbered clansmen and their crude modes of warfare didn't stand a chance against the sophisticated armies of England. Charles's Highland forces were massacred at the Battle of Culloden in 1746, and the victorious English marched through the north in a campaign of terror and revenge. The clans were disbanded, and with their passing, no shred of independent Scotland survived. And so a major wave of emigrants was born.

What the Irish call "seven hundred years of enslavement" began when Henry II of England led an army across the Irish Sea in 1171. The Irish Catholic Church at that time had remained stubbornly independent of Rome as well as of Canterbury, the seat of the Catholic Church in England. Pope Adrian IV, the only English pope, authorized Henry to bring Irish Catholics back to Rome and Canterbury. Once the English had gained a foothold in Ireland, Henry's conquering barons built castles and towns through the center and in the west of Ireland. Outside these English regions, Irish law and custom reigned, and there were frequent skirmishes between English and Irish forces.

Later, during the Reformation, Henry VIII tried to force the Irish Catholics to become Anglicans. But except for some of the nobility, the Irish would not embrace Henry's Protestant faith. Henry's forces invaded and subdued one chieftain after another and seized Catholic Church lands. Many sacred relics were destroyed, including the Staff of Saint Patrick, which was burned in a Dublin street. Henry had himself declared king of England and Ireland.

After Henry, Queen Elizabeth gave the captured Irish lands to English soldiers and settlers like Walter Raleigh. Although he never lived in Ireland, Raleigh left a lasting mark when his peasants began to plant a new vegetable—discovered by the expeditions he had sent to Virginia—the potato.

As they saw their lands falling into English hands, the Irish continued to rebel against the queen. One of the great Irish risings was led by Hugh O'Neill, the Earl of Tyrone. It ended when O'Neill surrendered in 1603, just four days after Elizabeth's death.

Tyrone was a county in Ulster, the northern region of Ireland. James I then seized over a half million acres of Ulster territory and gave it to English and Scottish settlers. He wanted to be sure that Protestant, pro-English control would remain strong in Ireland. Most of the new landowners were Scotch

Presbyterians, who took the best land. The Scotch-Irish set their feet firmly on Irish soil and kept their hearts dedicated to English rule.

Despite the wars and the confiscations of land, Irish resistance did not die. The Irish held firm to the Catholic Church and refused to regard themselves as English subjects. So the wars continued, and the confiscations continued, and in their wake law upon law stripped the Irish of their civil and religious liberties.

In 1649 Oliver Cromwell, who had led the revolution against King Charles I, invaded to punish an Irish rebellion. The cities fell to his armies, who massacred the citizens—men, women, and children. One third of the Irish people died during the Cromwell campaign, either as victims of the war or of the famine and disease that followed. To this day the Irish regard Cromwell as the greatest villain in English-Irish history.

The last stand of the Irish came forty years later. After James II was deposed, he fled to Ireland to raise a Catholic army, which he hoped would help him regain his throne. But his forces lost the Battle of the Boyne in 1690, and within a year Catholic resistance to William III was crushed. An Irish poet, Egan O'Rahilly, wrote this lament at that time:

Inis Fál

Now may we turn aside and dry our tears!
And comfort us! And lay aside our fears,
For all is gone!

All comely quality!
All gentleness and hospitality!
All courtesy and merriment

Is gone!
Our virtues, all, are withered every one!
Our music vanished, and our skill to sing!

Now may we quiet us and quit our moan!
Nothing is whole that could be broke; No thing
Remains to us of all that was our own.[2]

(TRANSLATED BY JAMES STEPHENS)

The United Kingdom of Great Britain and Ireland
was born in 1801, when Ireland was officially joined
to England, Wales, and Scotland by the Act of
Union. Four kingdoms, four peoples, were now
united under the rule of one monarch and the government of one parliament. The English conquest of
the British islands was apparently complete. But
proud, distinct cultures remained in Wales, Scotland, and Ireland, and conflict and friction continued—indeed right down to the present-day out-
bursts of nationalism in each country. This would
contribute to the decision that many people made—
and would make—to emigrate to America.

Chapter 3

"Planting" the New World

Eastward Hoe!, a popular English play of the early seventeenth century, told of the glowing riches to be found in the New World:

> SEAGULL: I tell thee, gold is more plentiful there than copper is with us. . . . Why, man, all their dripping-pans and their chamber pots are pure gold . . . and, for rubies and diamonds, they go forth on holidays and gather 'em by the seashore, to hang on their children's coats. . . .[1]
>
> (Act III, Scene iii)

A flood of words was written in the same vein. John Smith, an English adventurer and explorer, argued the benefits of planting in the New World. What greater happiness can a man desire, he asked, than to tread and plant that ground that he hath purchased by the hazard of his life? . . . than planting and building a foundation for his posterity? . . . than to seek to convert those poor savages to know Christ and humanity? . . . [than] the discovering of things unknown, erecting towns, peopling countries . . . and gain to our mother country a kingdom to attend her and find employment for those that are idle, because they know not what to do?[2]

The same arguments that Richard Hakluyt had used to convince Queen Elizabeth were now being put forward to persuade the English people. And reports from America were persuasive, such as this one from Thomas Morton, who had gone to live in Mount Wollaston (later Quincy), Massachusetts:

In the month of June, 1622, it was my chance to arrive in the parts of New England with 30 servants and provisions of all sorts fit for a plantation. While our houses were building, I did endeavor to take a survey of the country. The more I looked, the more I liked it. And when I had more seriously considered of the beauty of the place, with all her fair endowments, I did not think that in all the known world it could be paralleled for so many goodly groves of trees, dainty fine round rising hillocks, delicate fair large plains, sweet crystal fountains, and clear running streams, . . . birds in abundance, fish in multitude. . . . If this land be not rich, then is the whole world poor.[3]

The people started to go. In 1705 Robert Beverley, the son of an English immigrant, described some of the first arrivals and the forces that drove them:

> This, as well as all the rest of the plantations, was for the most part at first peopled by persons of low circumstances, and by such as were willing to seek their fortune in a foreign country. . . .
>
> Those that went over to that country first were chiefly single men, who had not the encumbrance of wives and children in England. And if they had, they did not expose them to the fatigue and hazard of so long a voyage, until they saw how it should fare with themselves. . . .
>
> But the single men were put to their shifts. . . . They had no hopes but that the plenty in which they lived might invite modest women of small fortunes to go over thither from England. However, they would not receive any but such as could carry sufficient certificate of their modesty and good behavior. Those, if they were but moderately qualified in all other respects, might depend upon marrying very well in those days, without any fortune. Nay, the first planters were so far from expecting money with a woman, that 'twas a common thing for them to buy a deserving wife, at the price of 100 pound, and make themselves believe they had a hopeful bargain.[4]

But gradually the pattern of immigration changed. Later settlers were often people who were either prosperous or who were escaping persecution in England. Thus when Parliament rebelled against Charles I, the king's followers (Cavaliers) went to the New World to escape reprisals from Cromwell. In general the Cavaliers went to Virginia, famous for its royalist sentiments, and the Roundheads (or supporters of Parliament) went to Massachusetts where the Puritan Separatists, or Pilgrims, had gone. At the time of the Restoration of the Stuarts, many people left for Plymouth to avoid the king's resentment or to protect their religious beliefs.

Jamestown, Virginia, had attracted immigrants in search of riches, or at least comfort. But life during the early years of the colony was harsh. People didn't know how to get on in the wilderness nor with the Indians. The colony was governed by confusion and disorganization. There was hunger, illness, and death. The years 1609 to 1611, the worst for Jamestown, were called the starving time. In 1624 the members of the Virginia House of Burgesses who had survived those years recollected the horrors:

> The allowance in those times for a man was only eight ounces of meal and half a pint of peas for a day . . . moldy, rotten, full of cobwebs and maggots, loathsome to a man and not fit for beasts. [These] forced many to flee for relief to the savage enemy, who [put them] to sundry deaths as by hanging, shooting and breaking upon the wheel. And others were

forced by famine to filch for their bellies, of whom one, for stealing two or three pints of oatmeal, had a bodkin [dagger] thrust through his tongue and was tied with a chain to a tree until he starved. If a man, through his sickness, had not been able to work, he had no allowance at all; and so consequently perished many. . . . Being weary of life, they dug holes in the earth and hid themselves until they famished.

So lamentable was our scarcity, that we were constrained to eat dogs, cats, rats, snakes, toadstools, horsehides and what not. One man, out of the misery he endured, killing his wife, powdered [salted] her up to eat her, for which he was burned. Many, besides, fed on the corpses of dead men, and one who had gotten insatiable [for] that food could not be restrained, until such time as he was executed for it.[5]

Plymouth Colony experienced a similar "starving time" at first. William Bradford, who became the second governor of the colony in 1621, described the initial hardships in his history, *Of Plymouth Plantation*:

In two or three months time, half of their company died, especially in January and February, being the depth of winter, and wanting houses and other comforts, [and] being infected with the scurvy and other diseases which this long voyage and unaccommodated condition had brought upon them.

So as there died some times two or three a day in [this] time, of one hundred and odd persons, scarce fifty remained. And of these, in the time of most distress, there were but six or seven sound persons, who, to their great commendation . . . spared no pains, night or day, but with abundance of toil and hazard of their own health, fetched [the sick] wood, made them fires, [prepared] them meat, made their beds, washed their loathsome clothes, clothed and unclothed them.[6]

As the first winter passed, Indians who were friendly to the colonists showed them how to plant the native vegetables and cultivate the soil. Within a year of their landing, the settlers celebrated the first Thanksgiving. Edward Winslow, one of the leaders, wrote to a friend in England:

We set last spring some twenty acres of Indian corn, and sowed some six acres of barley and peas. And according to the manner of the Indians, we manured our ground with herrings . . . which we have in great abundance. . . . God be praised, we had a good [harvest] of Indian corn, and our barley [was fairly] good, but our peas [were] not worth the gathering, for . . . they were too late sown.

Our harvest being gotten in, our governor sent four men . . . fowling, so that we might . . . rejoice together after we had gathered the fruit of our labors. Those four, in one day, killed as much fowl as . . . served the company almost a week. At which time, . . . many of the Indians came among us, and among [them was] their greatest chief, Massasoit, with some ninety men, whom for three days we entertained and feasted. And they went out and killed five deer, which they brought to the plantation, and bestowed upon [us]. And although it be not always so plentiful as it was at this time with us, yet by the goodness of God, we are so far from want that we often wish you [were] partakers of our plenty.[7]

While the first colonists in Virginia had migrated mainly in search of economic gain, these first immigrants to Massachusetts were Pilgrims, who came to build a community where they could live according to their religious beliefs.

In England the Pilgrims had been known as the Separatists. They had left the Church of England because they believed the Anglican way of worship was too much like the Roman Catholic. The Separatists also rejected a state church, headed by the king, which dictated religious practice and policy for all congregations. The Separatists believed that each religious congregation should be independent and self-governing, but English law did not agree. It made membership in independent congregations punishable by imprisonment and forfeiture of property.

And so in 1608 a group of Separatists emigrated to Holland, where they hoped they could worship freely. But although they found religious freedom among the Dutch, they found it hard to be aliens. They were excluded from the craft guilds, and were hard-pressed to make a living. Furthermore, as Bradford noted, the young people were taking "extravagante and dangerous courses, getting the raines off their neks." The elders were afraid Dutch life might become too attractive to them. So in 1620 they organized the *Mayflower* voyage. William Bradford wrote:

> The place they had thoughts on was some of those vast and unpeopled countries of America which are plentiful and fit for habitation. . . . [Some], out of their fears, objected against [this proposal] . . . [alleging] it was subject to many inconceivable perils and dangers. . . .
>
> It was answered, that all great and honorable actions are accompanied with great difficulties, and must be both enterprised and overcome with . . . courage. It was granted the dangers were great, but not desperate; the difficulties were many, but not invincible.

The group decided to cross the ocean and embarked from Delftshaven, Holland, in late July 1620, and from Plymouth in September. According to Bradford:

> After they had enjoyed fair winds and weather for a season, they were encountered many times with cross winds and met with many fierce storms with which the ship was shroudly [wickedly] shaken, and her upper works made

very leaky; and one of the main beams in the midships was bowed and cracked, which put them in some fear that the ship could not be able to perform the voyage. . . .

But . . . after a long beating at sea, they fell with that land which is called Cape Cod. . . .

Being thus arrived in a good harbor, and brought safe to land, they fell upon their knees and blessed the God of Heaven who had brought them over the vast and furious ocean.[8]

The Pilgrims found Cape Cod desolate and severe. A month later they sailed west again and landed, on Christmas Day, at a more hospitable place. There they established Plymouth Plantation.

More colonies followed Jamestown and Plymouth. Many people were able to scrape together the money to make the voyage and establish themselves in Massachusetts and Virginia.

But for others, who found the costs were too high, the only way to emigrate was as indentured servants. This meant farmers in the Colonies paid the costs of bringing new immigrants over and promised to support them. In return the servant would work for the farmer from four to seven years. At the end of the servant's indenture, the farmer would give the person his or her freedom and some clothing, money, tools, and land.

John Hammond came to America in 1636 as an indentured servant. Twenty years later he wrote a pamphlet giving advice for people who wanted to come to the Colonies as indentured servants. He warned them to find out all they could about the persons to whom they bound themselves and to seek employers with honest reputations. He advised having contracts in writing, for an employer's spoken promise "to do this or that" was not legally binding. Hammond went on to say that the work was not as hard as in England:

> Little or nothing is done in wintertime. None ever work before sun rising nor after sunset. In the summer, they rest, sleep or exercise themselves five hours in the heat of the day. Saturday's afternoon is always their own, . . . and the Sabbath [is] spent in good exercises [religious worship].
>
> The women are not, as is reported, put into the ground work, but occupy such domestic employments and housewifery as in England, that is dressing victuals [preparing food], righting up the house, milking, employment about the dairies, washing, sewing, etc. And both men and women have times of recreations, as much or more than in any part of the world. . . .
>
> Those servants that will be industrious may, in their time of service, gain a competent estate before their freedoms, and those that appear so industrious gain esteem and assistance. There is no master almost but will allow his servant a parcel of clear ground to plant some tobacco in for himself, which he may husband at those many idle times [the master] hath allowed him . . . [and] which in time of shipping he may

[sell]. . . . He may have cattle, hogs, and tobacco of his own, and come to live gallantly. But this must be gained, as I said, by industry and affability, not by sloth nor churlish behavior.

. . . Such preferment hath this country rewarded the industrious with, that some [who were of low] employment in England, have there grown great merchants and attained to the most eminent advancements.[9]

But indentured servitude was often not as fair as Hammond made it sound. Many masters tried to squeeze as much work out of a servant as they could, and at as little expense to themselves as possible. A servant in Maryland, Elizabeth Sprigs, wrote to her father:

What we unfortunate English people suffer here is beyond the probability of you in England to conceive. . . . I, one of the unhappy number, am toiling almost day and night, . . . then tied up and whipped to that degree that you'd not serve an animal. [We have] scarce anything but Indian corn and salt to eat, and that even begrudged. Nay, many negroes are better used. [We are] almost naked, no shoes nor stockings to wear. And . . . after slaving during Master's pleasure, what rest we can get is to wrap ourselves up in a blanket, and lie upon the ground. This is the deplorable condition your poor Betty endures. And now I beg, if you have any bowels of compassion left, show it by sending me some relief. Clothing is the principal thing wanting.[10]

Many servants who experienced the kind of treatment Elizabeth Sprigs described rebelled in the only way they could—by running away. The masters would advertise for their return in the Colonial newspapers.

> Ran away some time in June last, from William Pierce of Nansemond County, . . . a convict servant woman named Winifred Thomas. She is [a] Welsh woman, short, black-haired, and young; marked on the inside of her right arm with gunpowder, W.T.[11]

> Run away from the subscriber, in Northumberland county, two Irish convict servants, named William and Hannah Daylies, tinkers by trade. . . . They had a note of leave to go out and work in Richmond county. . . . Soon after, I heard they were run away.[12]

But in spite of the hardships, immigrants continued to come to America from the British Isles.

Chapter 4

Not Only the English Come

As the Colonies grew, more non-English people from the British Isles began to arrive, though most of the immigrants in the seventeenth century were English. Many were debtors, punished for having no money to pay their bills. Some were convicts who were "transported" to America and forced to labor as servants as punishment for crimes. This was particularly true of the Irish, who often found themselves at odds with English rule and its laws in Ireland.

But many others came freely. At the end of the seventeenth century, Gabriel Thomas, a Welsh immigrant in Philadelphia, wrote that the poor could earn three times what they could make in England.

> The first was a blacksmith, me next neighbor, who himself and one negro man he had, got fifty shillings in one day, by working up a hundred pound weight of iron. . . .

And for carpenters, bricklayers, masons—
[any] of these tradesmen will get between five
and six shillings every day, constantly. As to
journeyman shoemakers, they have two shillings
per pair, both for men and women's shoes. And
journeymen tailors have twelve shillings per
week and their diet. . . . Potters have sixteen
pence for an earthen pot which may be bought
in England for four pence.[1]

The rude colonies had become prosperous towns
and cities. In Philadelphia, Gabriel Thomas wrote,
there were

> several good schools of learning for youth, [for]
> the attainment of arts and sciences, as also
> reading, writing, etc. Here is to be had on any
> day in the week, tarts, pies, cakes, etc. We also
> have several cooks shops, both roasting and
> boiling, as in the city of London. . . .
> All sorts of very good paper are made in the
> German Town, as also, very fine German linen,
> such as no person of quality need be ashamed
> to wear. And in several places, they make
> woolen cloth, the manufacture of all which
> daily improves. And in most parts of the
> country, there are many curious and spacious
> buildings, which several of the gentry have
> erected for their country houses.[2]

In the eighteenth century, about three hundred
thousand Scotch-Irish immigrants came to the
Colonies. They were descendants of the Scots whom

James I had invited to Northern Ireland in the early
seventeenth century to "defend the borders and
fortresses" against the Irish. A seventeenth-century
commentator noted that

> the parts of Scotland nearest to Ireland sent
> over abundance of people and cattle that filled
> the counties of Ulster that lay next to the
> sea. . . . [For] the most part, [they] were such
> as either poverty, scandalous lives, or at the
> best, adventurous seeking of better accommoda-
> tion sent that way.[3]

Despite such humble beginnings, the Scotch-Irish
made Ulster the most prosperous region in Ireland.
Their livestock and dairy trade flourished. The
woolen cloth they manufactured competed well
with English-made goods—in fact, too well. English
landlords and manufacturers pressed Parliament to
pass laws restricting Irish trade, which meant
Scotch-Irish trade. Irish exports to England, Scotland, and the American Colonies were severely cur-
tailed. The manufacture of woolen cloth was forbidden. For a while, the Scotch-Irish were allowed
to export raw wool to the continent of Europe, but
then this outlet, too, was barred. Jonathan Swift,
the author of *Gulliver's Travels*, who was born in
Ireland of English parents, wrote of Ulster in the
early eighteenth century that

> whoever travels through this country and ob-
> serves . . . the faces and habits and dwellings
> of the natives, would hardly think himself in a

land where either law, religion, or common
humanity was professed. . . . The old and sick
[are] every day dying and rotting by cold and
famine and filth and vermin. The younger
laborers cannot get work, and consequently
pine away for want of nourishment to a degree
that, if at any time they are accidentally hired
at common labor, they have not the strength to
perform it.[4]

Matters were soon made worse by crop failures. In
1728 Archbishop Boulter of Ireland, in a series of
letters to the Duke of Newcastle, reported that

the scarcity and dearness of provision still increases in the North. Many have eaten the oats
they should have sowed their land with. And
[unless] the landlords will have the good sense
to furnish them with seed, a great deal of land
will lie idle this year. . . .

The humor [inclination] of going to America
still continues, and the scarcity of provisions
certainly makes many quit us. There are now
seven ships at Belfast that are carrying off about
1000 passengers thither. And if we knew how
to stop them, as most of them can neither get
victuals nor work, it would be cruel to do it.

Nine months later he reported to the king again:

We have had for several years some agents
from the colonies in America, and several
masters of ships, that have gone about the
country and deluded the people with stories of

great plenty, and estates to be had for going for, in those parts of the world. And they have been the better able to seduce people by reason of the necessities of the poor of late.[5]

New England Puritanism was compatible with Scotch-Irish Presbyterianism, but New England's best land—which was never too good to begin with —was already occupied, so the Scotch-Irish went south to New Jersey, Pennsylvania, and the interior lands of the Carolinas. Robert Witherspoon, who went to South Carolina as a child in 1734, later wrote an account of his first impressions of life in the wilderness:

> My mother and we children were still in ex-pectation that we were coming to an agreeable place. But when we arrived and saw nothing but a wilderness, and instead of a fine timbered house, nothing but a mean dirt house, our spirits quite sank. . . .
>
> My father gave us all the comfort he could by telling us we would get all those trees cut down, and in a short time there would be plenty of inhabitants. While we were at this, our fire . . . went out. [Father went to a distant neighbor's to get fire.] We watched him as far as the trees would let us see, and returned to our dolorous hut, expecting never to see him or any human person more. But after some time he returned and brought fire. We were soon comforted, but evening coming on, the wolves began to howl on all sides. We then feared being de-

voured by wild beasts, having neither gun nor dog nor any door to our house.

But the Scotch-Irish immigrants soon adjusted to frontier conditions.

> After a season, some men got such a knowledge of the woods as to "blaze" paths [with axe marks on trees], so the people soon found out to follow "blazes" from place to place. . . . People were very strong and healthy. All that could do anything wrought diligently, and continued clearing and planting as long as the season would admit, so that they made provisions for the ensuing year.[6]

Dressed in fringed hunting shirts and breeches made of coarse cloth or leather, dangling Indian axes and knives from their belts, their feet clad in moccasins, the Scotch-Irish set a new style. Their houses were earthen-floored cabins, made of logs held together without nails, for there were none in the backwoods. Their entertainments—boxing and wrestling matches and other demonstrations of physical prowess— were considered rowdy and crude by the dwellers in the older towns and cities.

Surrounded in Ireland by hostile Catholics and harassed by England because they would not conform to the official church, the Scotch-Irish remained devoted to the Presbyterian Church. Their clergymen were well educated because it had been fairly easy for students to travel from Ulster to Scotland. If new Presbyterian ministers were to be well educated, and the Scotch-Irish insisted on this, some means of training them in America had to be devised. In 1728 William Tennent, a clergyman who had emigrated from Ulster, founded the first Presbyterian school at Neshaminy, Pennsylvania, which became known as the Log College. George Whitefield, an eminent evangelist, described the college in his personal journal in 1739:

> The place wherein the young men study now is . . . called The College. It is a log house, about twenty feet long, and near as many broad, and to me, it seemed to resemble the school of the old prophets, for their habitations were mean. . . . From this . . . place, seven or eight worthy ministers of Jesus have lately been sent forth. More are almost ready to be sent, and the foundation is now laying for the instruction of many others.[7]

Scotch-Irish Presbyterians soon founded Princeton (College of New Jersey), Dickinson, Washington and Jefferson, Allegheny, and Hampden-Sydney colleges.

By the mid-eighteenth century, Highland Scots began to join the migration to America. After the defeat of the Highland army of Bonnie Prince Charlie at Culloden in 1746, the conquering English army burned the people's houses and fields to punish the rebels. The wearing of the clan tartans was forbidden. Highlanders were not allowed to bear arms. Highland acreages were confiscated and given to English officers and soldiers. Hunters could no longer range freely over the hills, for a good deal of the land and the game was now private English property. A proud, independent people was being forced to conform to alien laws.

King George II offered to pardon any rebels who agreed to move to the Colonies, and so the Scottish migration began, with rebels, farmers, the down-and-out, and the disaffected. Some Lowlanders also joined the exodus, and some emigrants were people of means. The flow of people out of Scotland became so great that the English government grew worried. If Scotland were empty, who would do the work? In 1773 English customs officials interviewed Scottish emigrants to find out why so many were leaving.

> William Gordon . . . aged sixty and upwards, by trade a farmer, married, hath six children who emigrate with him. . . . Having two sons already settled in Carolina, who wrote him encouraging him to come there; and finding the rents of lands raised in so much that a possession for which his grandfather paid only eight marks Scots, he himself at last paid sixty; he was induced to emigrate. . . . His circumstances were greatly reduced not only by the rise of rents, but by the loss of cattle, particularly in the severe winter [of] 1771. . . . All these things concurring induced him to leave his own country in hopes that his children would earn their bread more comfortably elsewhere. . . .

Elizabeth McDonald, aged 29, unmarried, [a] servant . . . intends to go to Wilmington in North Carolina. Left her own country because several of her friends, having gone to Carolina before her, had assured her that she would get much better service and greater encouragement in Carolina than in her own country.[8]

Only the Irish (other than the Scotch-Irish) failed to emigrate in sizeable numbers during the eighteenth century, perhaps because the Colonies were too intensely Protestant. Yet some Irish had come as indentured servants. And Maryland, which was founded by Catholics, was a haven for any Irish person. But the great migration from Ireland would not come until a hundred years later.

The people in the Colonies owed their allegiance to England. They were governed by English laws. Their language was the language of England, and many of their customs were derived from English ways. Yet in the decades before the Revolution, despite the brewing storm over what the colonists called their "rights as Englishmen," the American character became increasingly un-English. English, Scots, Scotch-Irish, Irish, and Welsh lived and worked together to a degree unknown in the British Isles. And living and working with them by now were people of many other nationalities—Dutch, German, French, Scandinavians, to name the more prominent "minorities," not to mention the native-American Indians. This multiethnic mix could hardly be called English. The colonists were turning into Americans, a diverse people loyal to their new locales to the point of chauvinism.

Dr. Alexander Hamilton* was born in Scotland and emigrated to Maryland. In 1744 he took a tour of the northern colonies. He wrote in his travel journal:

> [Philadelphians] have in general a bad notion of their neighboring province, Maryland, esteeming the people a set of cunning sharpers. But my notion of the affair is that the Pennsylvanians are not a whit inferior to them in the science of chicane, only their method of tricking is different. A Pennsylvanian will tell a lie with a sanctified, solemn face; a Marylander, perhaps will convey his fib in a volley of oaths. But the effect and point of view is the same, though the manner of operating be different.

Moving on to New York, Dr. Hamilton gave his readers a taste of the ethnic variety in the city:

> There is a spacious church belonging to the English congregation, with a pretty high but heavy, clumsy steeple . . . fronting the street called Broadway. There are two Dutch churches . . . at the head of Broadstreet. . . . The Jews have one synagogue in this city.[9]

England had planted the American Colonies, but once they were set into the soil, their growth was

---

* Not to be confused with the first secretary of the treasury, who was killed by Aaron Burr in a duel in 1804.

shaped by American conditions and concerns. Americans were a new kind of people, with different loyalties and goals from those of the English who ruled them.

Benjamin Franklin, the son of an English immigrant, had already described some of the differences between American and European values in 1750 in a pamphlet:

> [It is not] advisable for a person to go [to America] who has no other quality to recommend him but his birth. In Europe it has indeed its value; but it is a commodity that cannot be carried to a worse market than that of America, where people do not inquire concerning a stranger, *What is he?* but, *What can he do?* If he has any useful art, he is welcome; and if he exercises it, and behaves well he will be respected by all that know him; but a mere man of quality who, on that account, wants to live upon the public, by some office or salary, will be despised and disregarded.[10]

Franklin set down the principle that had made the Colonies a new world indeed.

Chapter 5

The English Colonies Become the American Nation

The Seven Years' War in North America was part of a struggle between England and France, fought in North America, Europe, and India. When it was over in 1763, England had gained control of India and vast American territories—Canada, Florida, several West Indian islands—as well as undisputed control of the area between the Appalachians and the Mississippi, which had formerly belonged to France and her ally, Spain.

England was now at the head of a vast empire, and needed a new policy to make its colonies subservient to the needs of the empire. This policy, known as imperialism, meant instituting tighter controls over colonial governments and regulating their trade for the advantage of England. England taxed the colonists and sent troops to guard its interests. To the English this policy made good sense. To the American colonists, it was an outrage.

For 150 years England had left its North American subjects free to develop their own way of life and government. They had set up Colonial assemblies and had elected men to represent them. The colonists' emotional ties with England had weakened. Some colonists of English descent were as much as three or four generations removed from regarding England as home. And since most English immigrants had come to America to escape economic hardship or political and religious oppression in England, their love for England was not great. This was even more true of the colonists whose roots were in Scotland, Wales, and Ireland. Furthermore, by the middle of the eighteenth century, the Dutch who had settled New Amsterdam had been absorbed into the English Colonies. And new arrivals from continental Europe were being integrated into the Colonial population. These people had no ties to England.

Radical ideas were taking hold in the American mind. Glimmerings of a democratic society could be discerned in the American belief that what a person did determined a person's merit, as Benjamin Franklin had written. New England town meetings, which all town residents could attend, and Colonial assemblies, whose members represented the particular towns or districts which elected them, had given Americans a taste for governing themselves. England was introducing imperial laws and policies that would deeply affect American life without regard to the colonists' views on these issues. As a result, Americans began to judge England less by what it was—their sovereign—than by what it did —dictate tyrannical laws.

Suddenly there were higher taxes and duties on tea, sugar, and a host of other goods imported into America. There was a new tax in the shape of a stamp that had to be purchased and put on newspapers, pamphlets, mortgages, calendars, and other printed documents. The colonists were forced to take English troops into their houses and inns. The traditional English laws guaranteeing the rights of a person accused of a crime were suspended. Uncooperative Colonial assemblies were dissolved. The list of abuses went on.

Benjamin Franklin prepared a witty and telling response to these acts in his pamphlet, *Rules by Which a Great Empire May Be Reduced to a Small One*, written in 1773.

> Take special care [that] the provinces . . . do not enjoy the same common rights, the same privileges in commerce [as in England]; and that they are governed by severer laws, all of your enacting, without allowing them any share in the choice of the legislators. . . .
>
> You are to suppose them always inclined to revolt, and treat them accordingly. Quarter troops among them, who by their insolence may provoke the rising of mobs. . . .
>
> In laying . . . taxes, never regard the heavy burdens those remote people already undergo,

in defending their own frontiers, supporting their own provincial government, making new roads, building bridges [etc.]. . . .

Think nothing of the wealth [your] merchants and your manufacturers acquire by the colony commerce . . . and the employment and support of thousands of your poor by the colonists. . . . But remember to make your arbitrary tax more grievous to your provinces by public declarations importing that your power of taxing them has no limits.[1]

Franklin expressed the sentiments of many Americans. These same points became the basis for the Declaration of Independence three years later.

By the time Franklin wrote his *Rules*, many people were entertaining the radical idea of independence from England, an idea that struck at the roots of governing. Monarchies were powerful. The idea that ordinary people could govern themselves was an idle daydream: impossible. But the radicals dared not strike yet. Colonial opinion had to be led gradually to so extreme a notion as independence. The radicals began to flout English laws, hoping the English would retaliate. If English oppression increased, more Americans would come around to the radical point of view. The strategy began to work. The English imposed harsher penalties on uncooperative colonies. After the 1773 Boston Tea Party, Boston Harbor was shut down and Massachusetts town meetings were suspended. Americans felt the weight of ever more arbitrary and oppressive laws. Then English troops fired on gatherings of colonists in Boston. There were riots.

Revolutionary propagandists churned out a flood of literature to woo the uncommitted to their camp. One of the most influential pamphlets was *Common Sense*, written by Tom Paine, a recent immigrant from England. Published early in 1776, the pamphlet argued that England was *not* the "mother country" of the colonists.

> Europe, and not England, is the parent country of America. This new world has been the asylum for the persecuted lovers of civil and religious liberty from every part of Europe. Hither have they fled, not from the tender embraces of the mother, but from the cruelty of the monster. . . . Not one third of the inhabitants are of English descent. Wherefore I [reject] the phrase of parent or mother country applied to England only, as being false, selfish, narrow, and ungenerous.[2]

In April 1775 a skirmish between English troops and the colonists occurred in Lexington, Massachusetts, and the first blood was shed in the War for Independence. The Second Continental Congress, composed of members from all the Colonies, went into its second year of session in Philadelphia in the summer of 1776. By now, revolutionary sentiments were respectable and supported by a majority of the delegates to the assembly. The members agreed to separate from England, and the Declaration of Independence was born. As John Adams pointed out in an article he wrote many years later, the Revolution began

> before the war commenced. The Revolution was in the minds and hearts of the people.[3]

There were, though, hearts and minds that had not been won over to the revolutionary cause. Many Scots who were fairly recent arrivals were still loyal to the Crown. Devout Anglicans believed they owed allegiance to King George III, who was head of the Church as well as monarch. Officials who had been appointed by George III tended to remain loyal, as did many landowners whose estates had been granted by the monarch. Many merchants who had ardently agitated against British restriction of trade still preferred the rule of England to control by revolutionary "mobs." One fourth to one third of the colonists remained loyal to England; they were known as Loyalists or Tories.

But in all but two of the states, as the Colonies were now called, loyalty to England was a crime. The eleven states passed laws limiting the Loyalists' freedom of speech and action. They could not vote and the states confiscated their property. The rebels, now known as patriots, damned the Loyalists for treason. The war had been going on for three years when the *Pennsylvania Packet* printed this attack on the Loyalists.

> Who were the occasion of this war? The Tories! Who persuaded the tyrant of Britain to

prosecute it in a manner before unknown to civilized nations, and shocking even to barbarians? The Tories! . . . Who advised and who assisted in burning your towns, ravaging your country, and violating the chastity of your women? . . . Who are the occasion of the thousands you now mourn the loss of? . . . Who have always counteracted the endeavors of Congress to secure the liberties of this country? . . . Who hold a traitorous correspondence with the enemy [and] . . . daily send them intelligence? . . . In short, who wish to see us conquered, to see us slaves . . . ? The Tories! . . .

Awake, Americans, to a sense of your danger. No time to be lost. Instantly banish every Tory from among you. Let America be sacred only to freemen. Drive far from you every baneful wretch who wishes to see you fettered with the chains of tyranny. Send them where they may enjoy their beloved slavery to perfection—send them to the island of Britain. . . . Banishment, perpetual banishment, should be their lot.[4]

Approximately one hundred thousand Tories took the hint. They left the United States, bound mostly for Canada or Britain.

Five years after the Colonies declared their independence, the war ended with the surrender of the British General Charles Cornwallis at Yorktown.

The leaders of the struggle for independence now

set upon the task of establishing the government and laws of the new nation. In the debate over immigration at the Constitutional Convention, some urged that immigrants, who would necessarily have "foreign attachments," be discouraged from coming, and that they be barred from serving in Congress. The more liberal camp argued that immigrants should be welcome, and that after a reasonable period, be granted all rights of citizenship, including serving in government. Speaking for the immigrant, James Wilson, a delegate and an immigrant (from Scotland), said that

> Not being a native . . . if the ideas of some gentlemen should be pursued, [the immigrant would be] incapacitated from holding a place under the very Constitution which he had shared in the trust of making. . . . [He remarked on] . . . the discouragement and mortification [foreigners] must feel from the degrading discrimination now proposed.[5]

In the end, the Constitution stipulated that foreign-born people could serve in Congress after a specified period of residence, though they would not be eligible for the presidency. Future laws regulating immigration and naturalization were left to Congress to make.

But it was not long before Congress exercised this power in passing the first of what would be many laws that discriminated against foreigners in America. Having just suffered a revolution themselves, the new Americans feared the possibility of another. The Alien and Sedition Acts, passed in 1798, reflected the anxiety felt by the Federalist party (which had argued the hardest line against immigration at the Constitutional Convention) over the revolutions and political turmoil that were shaking Europe. The French had overthrown their monarchical government in 1789, executed their king, and were spreading a revolutionary ideology throughout Europe. In 1798 the Irish had risen against England. Political exiles from Ireland and the Continent were suspected of bringing radical ideas and foreign influence with them. In response, the Alien and Sedition Acts increased the residence requirement for naturalization from five to fourteen years. These acts also gave the President the power to order the deportation of "such aliens as he shall judge dangerous to the peace and safety of the United States." Rarely has legislation so reflected the views of one political party. It underlined the traditional Federalist stand against the Republican view of a more democratic, broad-based citizenry. But it wasn't long before the Republicans struck back.

In the election of 1800 the votes of the various ethnic communities in the United States helped defeat the Federalist party, and it started its slide into oblivion. But distrust of foreigners, which was so much a part of Federalist thinking, did not disappear. It would crop up over and over again, particularly as greater waves of immigrants than any American in the year 1800 could have imagined broke on the nation's shores in the coming century.

Chapter 6

British and American Cousins

The United States began keeping records of entering immigrants in 1820, and by 1930, approximately four and a quarter million people had emigrated from England, Scotland, and Wales. British immigrants were the newcomers to America who most easily fitted in despite the political enmity that remained between the two nations. The predominant culture of the United States was, and to a considerable degree still is, essentially British—white, Anglo-Saxon, Protestant.

British immigrants looked like Americans, they spoke the same language, shared the same faiths. The American legal system was based on British common law. The way of life in the two countries was similar, except for the elaborate and rigid British class structure. The terms "our British cousins" and "our American cousins" were bandied about on either side of the Atlantic, expressing the links between British and American cultures.

51

During the nineteenth century the British kept coming in a steady stream. Each new generation joined the Americans in shaping the great movements of that era: the settling of the western frontier and industrialization. Their experiences were very much like those of the native-born. And yet they were different, for despite the compatibilities, the British were nevertheless immigrants. They experienced, with other immigrants, the wrenches of leaving home, the arduous ocean passages, the fears and joys that came with starting lives anew in a new land.

American industries were thriving, now that the United States no longer depended on "family" trade with England for manufactured goods. With the Louisiana Purchase in 1803, the landmass controlled by the United States doubled in size. There was more land than Americans could conceivably settle and cultivate themselves, more human labor needed to build business and industry than the population could provide. There was not only room for immigrants to run the factories, build the cities, and work the land, there was a need for them.

At the same time, Britain was bursting at the seams. Its population was increasing rapidly. The supply of labor far exceeded the demand for it, and an outlet was needed for the surplus. Also, while the United States was expanding its economy and increasing its territory, equally momentous developments were taking place in Britain: "revolutions" in agriculture and industry. These would create new classes of immigrants who would rush to meet America's needs.

Until the late eighteenth century, British farmers had worked the land in much the same way as their ancestors in the Middle Ages. Farmers cultivated strips of land scattered among various open fields, rather than single, enclosed plots. They used ancient tools, the spade, hoe, sickle, and wooden plow. Each rural family had the right to graze its livestock on common pastures and to gather firewood from common land. The agricultural system was inefficient, but it provided an adequate, if crude, livelihood.

This began to change toward the end of the eighteenth century. Some larger landowners started to experiment with advanced methods of farming and animal husbandry. New inventions, like the horse-drawn drill seeder, could far outstrip a farmer sowing seed by hand. Landowners rotated crops and used fertilizers to increase the harvests. They attempted to improve their livestock by selective breeding.

This kind of agriculture required using land in a way that was at odds with the old system. At the urging of the progressive and generally prosperous landowners, Parliament enacted further enclosure laws, which broke up the open-field system. Land commissions assigned farmers plots of land, which the new owners then enclosed by fences or hedges. Sheep owners took much of the land for pasture. Small farmers often ended up with less land than before, and some, who could not produce proof of their rights to the fields they had been working, got no land at all. The poorest villagers, who had relied on grazing their small stock on the commons, now had no pasture. And as the land became more productive with new machines and methods, fewer laborers were needed to work it.

Industry, too, was transformed. Until the late eighteenth century most industries were "cottage industries." Spinners, weavers, potters, metal-workers, and other artisans generally worked in their homes or in small village shops. But then new inventions changed all that. The spinning jenny and the power loom gave birth to the textile mill. Advances in iron-smelting technology and the invention of the steam engine created whole new kinds of industrial enterprises. And to power the blast furnaces and the engines that drove the factory machines, the steamships, and the railroads, Britain needed to extract the coal and metal ores buried in its soil. The workplace was transformed from the cottage and shop to the factory and the mine.

Quiet, green rural England was changing into an ugly industrial landscape. In his novel, *Hard Times*, Charles Dickens described the kind of English town that had become common by 1850.

> It was a town of red brick, or of brick that would have been red if the smoke and ashes had allowed it; but as matters stood it was a town of unnatural red and black like the painted face of a savage. It was a town of

machinery and tall chimneys, out of which
interminable serpents of smoke trailed themselves forever and ever, and never got uncoiled.
It had a black canal in it, and a river that ran
purple with ill-smelling dye, and vast piles of
buildings full of windows where there was a
rattling and a trembling all day long, and where
the piston of the steam-engine worked mo-
notonously up and down like the head of an
elephant in a state of melancholy madness.[1]

Although the Industrial Revolution produced
greater work opportunities for the laboring class and
provided a better income for some than they had
made at the home loom or forge, it rang the death
knell for the independent artisan. Workers were
now dependent on industrialists for their livelihood,
and industrialists made the most of this dependence
by exploiting their laborers. Fourteen- to sixteen-
hour workdays were common for adults and children. The poet William Blake described the foul,
noisy, ill-ventilated factories as "dark, Satanic
mills." The mines were all this and dangerous, too.
Wages for backbreaking work were scarcely enough
to keep up with the rising costs of bread and meat.
Periodic depressions left great numbers of industrial
workers without a source of livelihood.

America, with its vast lands, offered hope for a
better life. The skills industrial workers were learn-
ing in British mills and mines were also needed in
young American industries. The United States had
so much growing to do—in industry, transportation,

and in developing its towns and cities—that its economy seemed to be immune from the boom or bust cycles of Britain. The United States had no permanent working class, in the European sense, where the children of laborers could only be laborers. A laborer in America could work his way up—become a foreman or an entrepreneur. The children of miners or factory workers could become lawyers or doctors.

But the many poor in England could rarely find the means to go to America. In the early years of the nineteenth century, most of the immigrants from Britain had owned small farms or been tenant farmers who wanted to improve their conditions. It was not till the United States entered the industrial age in full force that waves of factory workers and miners would join them.

Rebecca and Edward Burlend, who went to Illinois in 1831, were typical farming immigrants. Mrs. Burlend wrote:

> In the year 1817 we took a small farm at a village in Yorkshire on a lease for fourteen years. . . . The rent was fixed at too high a rate for us to obtain a comfortable livelihood. We did indeed, by . . . great industry and strict economy, maintain our credit to the end of the lease. But the severe struggles we had to endure to meet our payments, . . . and the entire absence of any prospects of being able to supply the wants of a large family . . . tended . . . to fix my husband's purpose of trying what

could be done in the western world. We accordingly disposed of our little furniture, settled our . . . affairs, and ultimately began our long journey the last week in August, 1831.

Leaving one's native country is painful. Rebecca Burlend set down her family's thoughts about emigrating:

It was at Liverpool, when we had got our luggage to a boarding house and were waiting the departure of a vessel, that the throes of leaving England and all its endearments put our courage to a test. . . . A stranger would have thought us a most unsocial family, as we sat in profound silence for an hour together. Only now and then a sigh would escape us. . . . Even our children . . . seemed to lose their . . . vivacity. My dear husband, who before had displayed nothing but hardihood, on this occasion had almost played the woman. After a deep silence, I not unfrequently observed his eyes suffused with tears, which though unnoticed by him, fell . . . down his sunbrowned cheeks. We were six days in this abode, and I may venture to assert that he did not spend six hours of the time in the forgetfulness of sleep. . . .

At last the day dawned on which we were to embark. . . . In twelve hours more, we should be on the deep . . . that morning he addressed me in the following manner: "O Rebecca, I cannot do it, I cannot do it! For myself I fear nothing; but the . . . uncertainty attending this step completely bewilders me. Should anything befall me, what will become of you and my children on the stormy ocean, or in a strange land and among pathless woods. Bad as our prospects are in England, we must go back! Such another night as the last has been I cannot survive! This terrible suspense and anxiety tears me in pieces."

Silently they began to gather their luggage together to return home. But Mrs. Burlend could see that her husband was not happy about his new decision, and that he needed encouragement and reassurance.

"I admit, my dear husband, that our situation is a very trying one. But remember how often and how long you have resolved to go to America. . . . You have adopted emigration only from a conviction that it would tend to the good of the family; and the Almighty is as able to preserve us and our children across the seas or in America as he is in England. Besides, if we return, we have broken up our home and sold our furniture, and should be worse situated than ever. Let us . . . go, and look to Providence for success."

The above advice on my part operated like a charm. . . . His answer was rather in deed than in word. In two hours more, our luggage was removed from the wagon . . . [and back] to the ship in which we had taken our berths.[2]

The tale was the same for many: They would not have left home if they could have done well there. James Rous, another English immigrant, wrote from his 165-acre farm in America in 1817:

> You can ask if we like it here as much as in our native land, to which I answer, that were I sure of a good life in England and a good prospect for my children, I should prefer the company of my old friends and native place. But . . . here . . . a man may soon get a good farm of his own, and may be as independent as your country squires, but not quite so lazy.[3]

In a letter to his parents in 1832, Thomas Morris, an immigrant from Lancashire to Ohio, wrote:

> I . . . am very glad to hear that you and all our brothers and sisters are in good health. And thank God we are the same. . . . I am very sorry that you are yet in an oppressed country. It is a pity that such a . . . sensible, good-looking boy as Thomas, my nephew, is, should be kept to the loom every day, and . . . every night too almost, while boys in this country of 15 or 16 years old are going to school.
>
> If you can by any means get as much as will buy your sea [provisions] and pay your passage over, I would advise you and my mother and [my brother] William to come, the sooner the better. You never had [as] good a chance in your life. . . . If you will come to us, I can

promise you shall never want common neces-
saries of life while I have health to raise them
off my own land. You used to say you would
like to occupy land of your own. If you will
come to me, you may have as much as you can
make use of. . . . You may think you are too
old, but there was older looking men and
women than you [on the ship] with us, and
[they] did very well. So now I will invite you
tenderly to embrace the opportunity and make
a start.

Morris went on to dismiss the efforts being made in
England to bring about social and economic reform.

You talk of better times in England and a
reform bill. But I see in my newspaper that
the [House of] Lords rejected the bill, and
disturbances and mobs began and are still
increasing.[4]

In America reform did not concern the immigrants.
They had found social and economic equality, as
their letters home indicate.

Philadelphia, 2nd November 1817
. . . The land is rich indeed, and every industrious farmer may become a freeholder in the
United States by paying eighty dollars, [as] the
first installment for a quarter of a section of
land. . . . The land being his own, there is no
limit to his prosperity. No proud tyrant can
lord it over him. . . . No game, timber, or fish-
ing laws to dread. Few and small taxes to pay.

. . . May the father of the human race pour down abundant blessings upon the authors . . . of such a benevolent system. . . .

MATTHEW FARRAR

New York, 27th March, 1818

. . . In this country the rich don't call the industrious people the "swinish multitude." The judge of the district, the justice of the peace, and the parson of our parish, are all pleased to pay, and receive visits from us. . . .

There are poor people here, but no hungry children crying for bread in vain. They have all enough, and to spare. This is the promised land, flowing with milk and honey. . . .

LUKE BENTLEY

Paterson, New Jersey, 4th May 1818

. . . No fawning, cringing adulation here. The squire and the mechanic converse as familiarly as weavers do in England. We call no man master here.

It is very distressing to hear that my old neighbors are working for six or eight shillings a week, while we [grumble] at thirty or forty.

I hope this [letter] will find all my old friends in good health, though I know it will find many of them poor. Tell them I should like to see them all here. . . .

DANIEL RIDGEWAY[5]

Chapter 7

Crossing the Atlantic and Getting Settled

So the British came. The first step was making the decision to leave home. The second was making the passage. The journey to America was so filled with perils that it is hard to say which of these steps was the more difficult.

Nineteenth-century immigrant vessels were not passenger ships as such. The transportation of immigrants across the Atlantic was, in fact, a by-product of trade. Merchant ships sailed to Britain from North America, bringing cotton and tobacco from the United States and timber from Canada. Their holds were often less than half full with British goods on the return trip. To increase the profits of the voyage, shipowners needed to acquire additional cargo in Britain. Many chose to carry human beings—immigrants.

Few immigrants could afford first- and second-class cabins; most sailed in steerage—large holds under the decks which had carried freight on the voyage over. The steerage holds were rudely fixed to accommodate the passengers. Rough, narrow planks were their berths, one berth crowded hard upon the next. The first immigrants traveled under sail, vulnerable to winds and weather. The voyage generally took about six weeks, but bad weather could double the time. The introduction of the steamship in the 1850s reduced travel time, and the new ships provided somewhat better accommodations, with better light and ventilation. But no immigrant in steerage ever traveled in comfort.

When immigrants booked their passage, they usually made arrangements through shipping brokers. Many brokers sold space they were not authorized to sell, and on attempting to board ships, emigrants found they had been tricked. British guidebooks warned emigrants to be on the watch for swindlers:

> Make your bargain for your passage with the *owner* of the ship, or some well-known respectable broker or ship-master. Avoid by all means those crimps [con men, hustlers] that are generally found about the docks and quays near where ships are taking in passengers. Be sure the ship is going to the port you contract for, as much deception has been practiced in this respect. It is important to select a well-known captain and a fast sailing ship, even at a higher rate.[1]

In 1854 Samuel Sidney, publisher of an English magazine that gave advice to would-be emigrants, appeared before a committee of Parliament that was investigating emigrant ships. Sidney described the act of booking passage as virtually an act of faith:

> It is just like taking a ticket on a railway in which you have never seen the carriage. You do not see anything of it until you are going in it, and then . . . it is too late to find fault.
>
> No doubt [it is a fraud]. [The brokers] are like recruiters. They collect emigrants. Their ships are known in the trade by the name of paper ships.[2]

The docks of Liverpool, which was the main port of embarkation for British emigrants, swarmed with robbers and tricksters. William Chambers, a Scottish journalist, advised emigrants of the 1850s to travel light, for they would have to guard their luggage at all times:

> If an emigrant knew the consequences, he would prefer going without a change of under-clothing for a month, rather than embarrass himself with baggage. I could not but pity the lot of many who fell in my way on the wharfs and in the railway stations. There they sat, each on a great box, unable to stir. They could not safely leave this precious encumbrance, and were as good as nailed to the spot.[3]

In the course of the century the British and American governments increased their regulation of the immigrant traffic. Sanitation and health requirements were imposed. But, especially in the earlier

years, medical examinations of emigrants, intended
to prevent outbreaks of disease on the ships, were
often perfunctory. Vere Foster, an emigrant in the
year 1850, described his physical examination in
Liverpool.

> I passed before [the government doctor] for
> inspection. He said without drawing breath,
> "What's your name? Are you well? Hold out
> your tongue. All right," and then addressed
> himself to the next person.[4]

Because most of the emigrant ships were cargo
vessels, their captains often would not let the
passengers board until the cargo had been loaded.
Frequently there was little time between the loading
of the cargo and a favorable tide. Dr. John Lan-
caster, a medical officer at the Liverpool emigration
station in the 1850s, had the opportunity to watch
thousands of emigrants embark. He described the
general disorder of the scene to a parliamentary
committee:

> We sometimes have dreadful scenes. . . . You
> may see men, women, and children clambering
> up the sides of the ship. . . .
>   Very often, when [the ship] gets to the
> entrance to the dock where it is very narrow,
> she is detained there for a short time while other
> vessels are going out, and during that time the
> passengers are scrambling in. I have seen 500
> or 600 men, women, and children in a state of
> the greatest confusion, and their screams are

fearful. On several occasions I have gone down and attempted to get on board, but I found it to be quite out of the question.[5]

When Vere Foster boarded his ship to America in 1850 he saw

men and women . . . pulled in any side or end foremost, like so many bundles. I was getting myself in as quickly and dextrously as I could, when I was laid hold of by the legs and pulled in, falling head foremost down upon the deck, and the next man was pulled down on top of me. I was some minutes before I recovered my hat, which was crushed as flat as a pancake.[6]

When the ships sailed down the river toward the ocean, the water was usually calm, and a breeze from the sea refreshed the passengers. They were on their way. But joy soon turned to distress. William Bell, who sailed with a group of fellow Scots in 1817, described the abrupt change:

The morning was fine, and the ebbing tide in a few hours carried us out of the river. During the day the wind, though light, continued favorable, and we had, literally speaking, a pleasure sail. Every heart was light and every face wore a smile. Some were reading the books they had the precaution to take along with them. Some [were] conversing about their prospects in America, or the friends they were leaving behind. And between decks, a party of young people were dancing a good part of the day. . . .

On the following morning, I was awakened at an early hour by the violent motion of the ship, and an unusual bustle on the deck. . . . A gale blew from the north-west. The sea roared and foamed around us, the passengers became sick, and everything began to wear a discouraging aspect. . . . Consternation and alarm were soon visible in every countenance. Children were crying, and women wringing their hands and wishing they had remained at home.[7]

In 1848 another immigrant, Henry Johnson, described a storm at sea six days before he arrived at New York:

Anything I have read or imagined of a storm at sea was nothing to this. . . . One poor family in the next berth to me whose father had been ill all the time of a bowel complaint I thought great pity of. He died the first night of the storm, and was laid outside of his berth. The ship began to roll and pitch dreadfully . . . the boxes and barrels, etc., began to roll from one side to the other. The men at the helm were thrown from the wheel, and the ship became almost unmanageable. At this time, I was pitched right into the corpse. The poor mother and daughter were thrown on top of us, and there, corpse, boxes, barrels, women and children all in one mess were knocked from side to

side for about fifteen minutes. . . . Shortly after
the ship got righted and the captain came down,
we . . . took [the body] on deck, and amid the
raging of the storm, [the captain] read the
funeral service for the dead and pitched him
overboard.[8]

But most of the squalor in steerage came from the
calculated acts of men. To make the voyages more
profitable, shipowners and captains spent as little as
possible on the comfort of steerage passengers.
Stephen de Vere, who sailed to America in 1847,
described the atmosphere belowdecks:

Hundreds of poor people, men, women, and
children, of all ages, from the drivelling idiot of
ninety to the babe just born, huddled together
without light, without air, wallowing in filth
and breathing a fetid atmosphere; sick in body,
dispirited in heart, the fevered patients lying
between the sound, in sleeping places so narrow
as almost to deny them the power . . . [to]
change . . . position.[9]

The diary of William Bell describes the food: "I have
never seen anything like [it] presented to humans."
The soup was "merely stinking water in which stinking beef had been boiled, which no dog would taste
unless he was starving." During a storm, when it
was impossible to prepare a hot meal, the only food
given to passengers was "rotten Dutch cheese, as
bitter as soot, and bread partly alive." Bell continued:

Many of our passengers were seized with a dysentery in consequence of eating putrid fresh beef—I mean [beef] that was fresh when we left Leith [in Scotland] five weeks ago. They were not allowed to taste it until it was unfit for use, and then they were made welcome to use it. Three or four seemed almost in a dying condition, and were placed under the doctor's care.[10]

When steamships shortened the voyage to about ten days, this was a blessing. According to two Welshmen who emigrated in the 1860s, conditions in steerage were not much improved, but the misery lasted a shorter time. John Owen wrote in 1867:

There were many unpleasant things, but the food was the worst. We had breakfast at eight o'clock, comprising tea and coffee every other day, [and] a warm loaf with a little butter. But that little was too much for me; its smell was enough, let alone its taste. At one o'clock two men came round with a jug of stew as if they were distributing it to pigs. Another brought bacon, another potatoes. The men looked as if they had not seen water for a month, and the desire for food was lost when we saw their hands. At six o'clock we had boiled water and treacle [molasses], instead of tea, with hard bread, and that is the kind of food we had on the voyage.

And, from John Davies in 1868, we learn that he

> left Liverpool aboard the *City of Baltimore*.
> . . . It was an iron vessel, strongly made, but
> one of the dirtiest I have ever been aboard. . . .
> The treatment received by the steerage pas-
> sengers is very poor. . . .
>
> It would be well for everyone to remember
> that all the room that a passenger can claim for
> himself is about two and a half feet in height,
> two feet wide, and six feet long, and in this
> small space he eats, lives, sleeps, etc. When it is
> mealtime, the steward comes past each man and
> gives everyone his share in his tin, in bed. It is
> the nearest thing in the world to feeding time
> at [an] animal show.[11]

Upon landing in New York, the early immigrants
had to contend with the same kind of free-for-all that
saw them off at Liverpool and other ports. Richard
Weston, who arrived from England in 1833, described the cold welcome that newcomers received:

> It was half-past ten before we arrived at the
> quay. Here we were landed in the dark, the rain
> pouring upon us, and our luggage strewed all
> around. The shops . . . were all shut, and we
> had no one to direct us where to proceed. We
> had therefore no alternative than to pass the
> night where we were, in the open air. . . . I
> constructed a barricade of the trunks belonging
> to myself and two fellow-passengers . . . over

which I put some [planks] which were lying
on the wharf. Under the lee of this shed, we
placed the female passenger who was ill of a
fever; and having procured a pitcher I pro-
ceeded into the town in search of water, and
some wine for the woman. This I procured
from a shop which I found still open, together
with a bottle of brandy and some cheese.
Myriads of rats kept squeaking and frisking
about and over us all night; one of them captured a piece of cheese from my knee while I
was at supper.

The next morning Weston went into the town to
look for a room.

On going along the quay, I passed two other
encampments of immigrants in Washington
Street. Some of them were lying huddled together under carts, some within the recesses of
doors, and some on the bare pavement. I en-
quired at a good-looking elderly woman who
was lying on the pavement—her head bare,
and her long grey hair fluttering in the breeze
—how long it was since she landed. She
answered . . . that it was six nights, and that
her party had lain all that time in the streets.[12]

The New York docks were crawling with swindlers
and thieves out to part immigrants from the money
and possessions they had brought with them. Besides having to protect themselves from thieves, the

new arrivals also had to be on the lookout for "runners," people employed by hotels and boarding-houses to drum up customers. One young immigrant in the 1840s was beset by two runners at once:

> The moment he landed, his luggage was pounced upon by two runners, one seizing the box of tools, the other confiscating the clothes. The future American citizen assured his oblig-ing friends that he was quite capable of carry-ing his own luggage. But no, they should relieve him . . . of that trouble. Each [represented] a different boarding house, and each insisted that the young Irishman . . . should go with him. . . . Not being able to oblige both gentlemen, he could oblige only one; and as the tools were more valuable than the clothes, he followed in the path of the gentleman who had secured that portion of the "plunder."[13]

It wasn't until 1855 that New York, the major port of entry, established an immigrant receiving station in Castle Garden at the Battery. Castle Garden pro-vided systematic handling of immigrants and lug-gage, and facilities for getting information, meeting family, changing money, and buying rail and boat tickets for travel inland.

For immigrants heading west from their ports of entry in the first quarter of the nineteenth century, the only way was overland by wagon or horseback or on foot. Morris Birkbeck, an English farmer heading for Illinois in 1817, described how some families made the trip:

A small wagon—so light that you might almost carry it, yet strong enough to bear a good load of bedding, utensils and provisions . . . —with two small horses, and sometimes a cow or two, comprises their all, excepting a little store of hard-earned cash for the land office of the district. . . . The wagon has a . . . cover, made of a sheet or perhaps a blanket. The family are seen before, behind, or within the vehicle, according to the road or weather, or perhaps the spirits of the party.

For others Birkbeck said:

A cart and single horse frequently affords the means of [transport], [or] sometimes a horse and a pack-saddle. Often the back of the poor pilgrim bears all his effects, and his wife follows, naked-footed, bending under the hopes of the family.[14]

Although it was never easy, the trip inland became less arduous after the opening of the Erie Canal in 1825, and after the introduction of steamboats and railroads in the 1830s and 1840s.

When they got there, immigrants found life on the frontier harsh, and many could not make the adjustment. William Faux was one of those who was bitterly disillusioned. In a letter to an English newspaper, which he wrote from Indiana in 1819, as he set out to emigrate back to his home, Faux urged his countrymen who could manage to live in some sort of comfort in England, "Stay where you are; for neither America nor the world have anything to offer you in return." To those who could not make do in England, he advised:

> If you come, come one and all of you, male and female, in your working jackets, with axes, ploughshares, and pruning-hooks in your hands, prepared long to suffer many privations. . . . I am now living on wild bucks and bears, mixed up and barbarizing with men almost as wild as they are . . . this is the lot of all coming here.[15]

Frontier life was especially difficult for women. They were often left alone, or with young children, while their men went off to hunt or trade. They had to endure dirt, disease, danger, and loneliness. A Welsh immigrant in Utah, "Jane," described her state in a letter to a friend back in Wales in 1862:

> I have seen little besides pain, sorrow, darkness and trouble. We are wearing out a miserable existence, anxiously looking for something we may never attain.
>
>   . . . The Indians have become very hostile and have attacked, robbed, wounded, and killed a great many. [My husband] is now hauling wood for winter use. He has to go a great distance and is away three days and two nights, sleeping under the wagon in danger of Indians, wolves, etc.
>
>   . . . The interior [of my log cabin] consists of a room seventeen feet long by sixteen feet

wide. In one corner is a fireplace, close by is a small window of six panes. Then comes my dining table . . . next comes my "wall of honor" where I have my pictures, books, *firearms*, and bed. A couple of chairs, a stool, boxes, and cradle complete the furniture of my room.

. . . I have four children, the two eldest are girls and the younger ones the other sort. . . . I will not describe our dress for fear you should think it some turn-out of the workhouse.[16]

People moving west found the Indians increasingly hostile. Many eastern Indians had been driven to new lands west of the Mississippi, yielding to President James Monroe's "removal" policy and the official Indian Removal Act of 1830 under Andrew Jackson. In their greed for new lands, white Americans ignored federal treaties, contemptuously expelled Indian landowners, abused the native Americans' human rights, and caused them untold hardship. The Plains Indians further west, who roamed with the buffalo and who were excellent fighters and marksmen with bow and arrow or with rifles, were a more formidable foe. From the beginning they fiercely resisted the encroachment on their grazing lands, streams, and beaver traps, marauding and killing cruelly. Only a few white trappers—of all backgrounds—gained their confidence. These men married Indian women and learned every stream and mountain in the Rockies. They would be the indispensable guides for the pioneers going to Oregon, Utah, and California.

So despite the fears and the hardships, most British immigrants felt they had made the right move. John Fisher wrote home from Michigan in 1833:

> I must give you my opinion of this country and draw some comparison between them. I have left England and its gloomy climes for one of brilliant sunshine and inspiring purity. . . . I . . . am in a country where all is life and animation, where I hear on every side the sound of exultation, where everyone speaks of the past with triumph, the present with delight, the future with growing and confident anticipation. Is not this a community in which one may rejoice to live? . . .
>
> The first [80 acre farm] I bought is worth nearly double the money I gave for it. The last . . . is worth five times what it cost. . . . I think if any of you, my brothers, think of farming you would do well in America.[17]

The United States remained a largely rural and agricultural society until the Civil War. Immigrant farmers from the British Isles helped to build the farming communities of the westward-moving frontier. After the Civil War, American industry started to grow on a small scale, and manufacturing was often combined with farming. An English immigrant, Edward Phillips, described this in a letter to his father in 1838:

I worked . . . at a great many factories for several hundred miles round [Cincinnati], and learned a little in every one until I got to be a good workman at weaving, spinning, carding, and dyeing. In 1833, I married and began to do a little business for myself. In 1835, I rented a farm . . . containing one hundred acres of land, with a small factory on it for carding wool for the country people. . . . I made a spinning machine, and looms, and [I] buy wool and make it into cloth of different kinds. I hire a hand to tend the carding machines and get my weaving done. I spin and prepare the yarn for the weaver. This is my employment for the present. The farm I get farmed on share, giving [the sharecropper] two thirds of the grain, and one half of the grass [in return] for the farming.[18]

So British immigrants also helped from such small beginnings to develop a primarily urban and industrial culture in the United States. Samuel Slater, for example, was one of the principal activists in the American Industrial Revolution. Slater brought the plans for the spinning jenny to the United States from England and founded the first American cotton thread factory in Pawtucket, Rhode Island, in 1793. Such immigrants who contributed important technical knowledge and operating experience in other fields, such as mining and metals, were delighted by how well they were able to live in America. Edward Kershaw, a weaver from Rochdale, England, who immigrated to Lynnfield, Massachusetts, in 1831 wrote home:

> I am between 20 and 30 pounds heavier than I was when I came to Lynnfield. . . . I never set me down to a meal but I think of the starving weavers of Rochdale.[19]

Many of these immigrants crossed the Atlantic during the periodic depressions in England. But even when times at home were good, the British came, because it seemed that opportunities in America were even better. They clustered where the work was, and formed large groups in the cotton and wool factories of New England, the silk mills of New Jersey, the coal mines of Pennsylvania and Illinois, the ore mines of Michigan, Montana, and Nevada.

The new British immigrants introduced more British ways and customs into the United States. Up to the nineteenth century, most Americans still held the Puritan distaste for treating a religious holiday with too worldly a celebration. But as time passed, Americans began to adopt the English way of keeping Christmas—singing carols, decorating a Christmas tree, and festooning their homes and churches with boughs of holly and fir. In sports the English introduced cricket and rugby to the playing fields of America. Scots ate oatmeal imported from Edinburgh, Dundee marmalade, and Lochfyne herrings. Welsh immigrants clung proudly to what they had preserved of the Welsh tongue during six hundred years of English domination. As late as 1891 Anne Williams expressed her feelings toward the language of her birthplace in a letter to a relative in Wales:

> I must ask pardon first for one thing, and that is I am not able to write a correct Welsh letter in return, so I will take the liberty of writing it in English. But now I don't wish you to carry the wrong idea and think I have forgotten my *Dear* Native *Language*, as I can speak that as good as ever and I am proud of it and I know I will never forget it and I like to read any Welsh letter. Yet I can't spell the words, so I always write in English.[20]

Because their native culture was compatible with that of the United States, English, Scottish, and Welsh immigrants faced fewer obstacles than did the Irish immigrants who were soon to come in large numbers.

Chapter 8

Ireland:
The Famine Years

After the United States won its independence, the numbers of Irish who emigrated to America began to increase. However, many still preferred to stay home: Why leave one Protestant-ruled land for another? The Irish had a powerful love for their land. They had suffered, bled, and died for Ireland during centuries of English rule. Few would leave until forced to. Even though conditions were bad in Ireland, there was hope they would improve.

After England crushed the Irish-Catholic army at the Battle of the Boyne in 1690, it had instituted a series of punishing laws called the Penal Code, which aimed to strip the Irish of virtually all civil rights. In their own country Irish Catholics were not allowed to vote, serve on juries, join the army or navy, carry guns, enroll in universities, teach school, become lawyers, or work for the government. It was forbidden to speak (or teach) the Irish language, Gaelic. Priests who were "troublesome" were deported. Irish Catholics were taxed to support the official Anglican Church.

The Penal Code remained in force for 125 years, and only slowly, and with much resistance, did Britain dismantle these laws during the nineteenth century.

Then, in 1815, it seemed as if the Irish might find an ally in Napoleon, for France and Ireland had a common enemy, England. But England defeated Napoleon at Waterloo, dashing Irish hopes for French aid and making England more powerful than ever. Politically, the Irish were now the most subjugated people in Europe. And so, after 1815, the numbers of emigrants to America increased. By the 1830s some fifty thousand Irish people were entering the United States each year.

In addition, the Irish population tripled between 1780 and 1840. The most densely populated country in Europe, Ireland could not house, feed, or provide work for the increasing numbers of its people. Except for the province of Ulster, Ireland had not been industrialized. Most Irish worked the land, but the land did not belong to them. English landlords owned it. These landlords often lived in fine houses in faraway London. They looked down on the Irish who worked their land and squeezed every bit of money from the people and the land that they could.

As the population and the demand for land increased, the landowners divided their estates into smaller and smaller farms. At the same time, they raised the rents. Many landlords threw their tenants off the land and converted their property into large farms and pastures that would yield bigger crops and beef and mutton for English tables and leather and wool for English factories. The poor began to fill the roads of rural Ireland and the streets of its cities in their search for a way to keep alive.

The Duke of Wellington, the British general who had defeated Napoleon at Waterloo, went on to become an important political leader. A native of Ireland, he had witnessed the distress of its population. In 1838 Wellington testified to the House of Lords, "There never was a country in which poverty existed to the extent it exists in Ireland." Nearly half of the rural families lived in windowless, one-room mud cabins. The potato, the North American vegetable that Sir Walter Raleigh had introduced to Ireland, was all that kept the Irish peasantry alive. A plot of an acre or so could yield enough potatoes to keep a family from starving, if not from hunger.

A British royal commission was appointed to investigate the Irish land system in 1843. Two years later it reported:

> It would be impossible to adequately describe the privations which [Irish rural families] habitually and silently endure . . . the laboring classes have [endured] sufferings greater, we believe, than the people of any other country in Europe have to sustain.[1]

A few months later Ireland fell into the grip of famine. It began in August 1845 with word from the Isle of Wight in the south of England that the potato crop there had been hit by a fungus that killed the plants. Would the English blight reach the fields of Ireland? All indications were that the Irish would be harvesting a bumper crop that year. The answer was not long in coming. In September the *Gardener's Chronicle* published the following announcement:

> We stop the Press with very great regret to announce that the potato Murrain [disease] has unequivocally declared itself in Ireland. The crops about Dublin are suddenly perishing . . . where will Ireland be in the event of a universal potato rot?[2]

Two years later a young Englishman doing relief work with the Society of Friends in Ireland, W. E. Forster, described the country's state as it went into its third year of famine:

> The town of Westport was in itself a strange and fearful sight, like what we read of in beleaguered cities; its streets crowded with gaunt wanderers, sauntering to and fro with hopeless air and hunger-struck look; a mob of starved, almost naked, women around the poor-house, clamoring for soup tickets.
> One poor woman whose cabin I had visited [in a rural district] said, "There will be nothing for us but to lie down and die." I tried to give her hope of English aid, but, alas! her prophecy has been too true. Out of a population of 240 I found thirteen already dead from want. The survivors were like walking skeletons—the men

> gaunt and haggard, stamped with the livid
> mark of hunger—the children crying with pain
> —the women in some of the cabins too weak to
> stand.[3]

The famine lasted four years, 1845 through 1848.
Although the crop of 1847 escaped the blight, so
few seed potatoes had been planted because of the
crop failures of the previous two years, that this good
crop was inadequate.

An Irish priest, Father Matthew, described the
blight in 1846:

> On the 27th [of July], I passed from Cork to
> Dublin, and this doomed plant bloomed in all
> the luxuriance of an abundant harvest. Return-
> ing on the third [of August], I beheld with
> sorrow one wide waste of putrefying vegetation.
> In many places the wretched people were seated
> on the fences of their decaying gardens, wring-
> ing their hands and wailing bitterly the destruc-
> tion that had left them foodless.[4]

This reappearance of the blight a second year dashed
all hopes. The winter of 1846–1847 was unusually
severe. In December 1846 Nicholas Cummins,
magistrate of Cork, toured the county. He described
the sufferings of the Irish in a letter to the Duke of
Wellington, which he also sent to *The Times* of
London for publication.

> In the first [hovel that I visited], six famished
> and ghastly skeletons, to all appearances dead,
> were huddled in a corner on some filthy straw.

. . . I approached with horror, and found by a low moaning they were alive. They were in fever, four children, a woman, and what had once been a man. . . . In a few minutes, I was surrounded by at least 200 such phantoms, such frightful spectres as no words can describe. . . . Their demoniac yells are still ringing in my ears, and their horrible images are fixed on my brain. My heart sickens at the recital, but I must go on.

. . . I found myself grasped by a woman with an infant just born in her arms and the remains of a filthy sack across her loins—the sole covering of herself and baby. The same morning, the police opened a house . . . which was observed shut for many days, and two frozen corpses were found, lying upon the mud floor, half devoured by rats. . . . In another house, within 500 yards of the cavalry station at Skibbereen, the dispensary doctor found seven wretches lying unable to move, under the same cloak. One had been dead many hours, but the others were unable to move either themselves or the corpse.[5]

Britain did not ignore the plight of Ireland. Officials in London provided cornmeal, soup kitchens, and public works employment programs. But the aid sent was little compared to what was needed. The British government believed it should not interfere in economic affairs, and it regarded Ireland's troubles as economic. Many Irish considered Britain's failure to provide enough aid during the famine years genocide, or the murder of a nation. Others saw Britain's behavior not as a malicious effort to destroy the Irish but only a continuation of the callousness and neglect with which it had governed Ireland for hundreds of years.

Then, in the winter of 1846–1847 epidemics of typhus and relapsing fever struck. Relapsing fever derived its name from the fact that patients would be subject to a series of severe attacks in the course of the illness. Victims of both illnesses suffered high fevers, vomiting, and delirium, as well as other symptoms. The Irish called the diseases famine fever, for the diseases were spread by lice, which abounded in the squalor of the famine years, and the weakened condition of the Irish made them vulnerable to infection.

In this dreadful winter of 1846–1847 the floodgates burst. Hope was gone; horror was everywhere. Great numbers of Irish gave up on Ireland and fled. Accurate figures on emigration are not available, but *at least* one million left during the famine years. More than half of the emigrants went to the United States; the rest went to England and Canada.

"All who are able are leaving the country," reported a British public works official in February 1847. Conditions on the famine ships were the worst ever known on the Atlantic crossing. Known as coffin ships, the vessels were horribly overcrowded and carried far too few provisions. "Famine fever" boarded the ships along with the passengers, and many who had escaped disease in Ireland were struck down during the crossing. Forty thousand or more died at sea or in quarantine in the United States and Canada in the year 1847 alone.

The word *decimated* means losing one out of ten people. Ireland was more than decimated in the famine years. Between 1845 and 1849 Ireland lost at least two and a half million out of a population of approximately nine million—a loss of slightly more than one out of every four people. At least one million of these emigrated. The rest died of starvation and disease.

Ireland's troubles did not end with the passing of the famine in 1849. Crop failures would recur, though never as sustained or devastating as in the 1840s. Landlords would maintain their stranglehold and continue to keep Irish farmers impoverished. British laws would continue to deny the Irish their basic civil and human rights. The system would not change until the establishment of the Irish Free State in 1921. And between 1846 and 1925, some four million Irish would emigrate to the United States.

Those who came in the nineteenth century arrived physically and mentally weakened. Exhausted from the privations they had experienced at home and during the crossing, they had neither the money nor the skills that could command much of an income. They settled in the back alleys, derelict buildings, and dank cellars of America's cities, notably Boston and New York.

The Irish became America's first ethnically distinct urban underclass, as black slaves had become the rural, racially different underclass. Native-born Americans despised the Irish because they were different in their ways and religion. They also competed against older Americans for jobs. Most national groups of immigrants that would come later to America would relive the pattern set by the Irish: being met with widespread hostility and discrimination and having to struggle to adapt to new conditions and to win acceptance.

t seemed wise for England to counter Spain's colonies by establishing her own. In 584 Queen Elizabeth gave Sir Walter Raleigh the authority and money to send out n expedition to America. ("Queen Elizabeth." Anonymous sixteenth-century engraving. Courtesy of the Prints Division, The New York Public Library.)

The next group of British immigrants to the New World arrived in 1607 at Jamestown in Virginia. (Plate from John Smith, "A True Relation . . ." London, 1607. Courtesy of the Rare Book Division, The New York Public Library.)

The Pilgrims organized the *Mayflower* voyage to America in 1620. They landed on Christmas Day and established Plymouth Plantation. ("Pilgrims Going to Church" by George Henry Boughton, 1867. Oil on canvas. Stuart Collection. Courtesy of The New-York Historical Society, New York City.)

England had planted the American Colonies, but once they were set to the soil, their growth was shaped by American conditions and concerns. Philadelphia, at the end of the eighteenth century. (William Birch, "Arch Street, with the Second Presbyterian Church," 1799. Colored etching with engraving from Birch's *The City of Philadelphia*. Courtesy of the Prints Division, The New York Public Library.)

COMMON SENSE;

ADDRESSED TO THE

INHABITANTS

OF

AMERICA,

On the following interesting

SUBJECTS.

I. Of the Origin and Design of Government in general, with concise Remarks on the English Constitution.

II. Of Monarchy and Hereditary Succession.

III. Thoughts on the present State of American Affairs.

IV. Of the present Ability of America, with some miscellaneous Reflections.

A NEW EDITION, with several Additions in the Body of the Work. To which is added an APPENDIX; together with an Address to the People called QUAKERS.

N. B. The New Addition here given increases the Work upwards of one Third.

Man knows no Master save creating HEAVEN,
Or those whom Choice and common Good ordain.
                                        THOMSON.

PHILADELPHIA PRINTED,

And SOLD by W. and T. BRADFORD. [1776]

Wrote by one Thomas Payne in the year 1776.

With the Louisiana Purchase in 1803, the landmass controlled by the United States doubled in size. There was not only room for immigrants, there was a need for them. (Edwin Whitefield, "View in the Backwoods, Ohio." Lithograph from *North American Scenery,* N.Y., 1846. Courtesy of The New-York Historical Society, New York City.)

Revolutionary propagandists churned out a flood of literature. One of the most influential pamphlets was *Common Sense*, written by Tom Paine, a recent immigrant from England. (Title page of *Common Sense,* 1776. Courtesy of The New-York Historical Society, New York City.)

In the nineteenth century, Americans began to adopt the English way of keeping Christmas, decorating a Christmas tree and festooning their homes and churches. ("The Christmas Tree." Wood engraving from *Harper's Weekly*, 1870. Courtesy of The New-York Historical Society, New York City.)

When steamships shortened the voyage to America to about ten days, this was a blessing. ("The British Steamer *Sirius*," 1838. Lithograph. Courtesy of the Stokes Collection, The New York Public Library.)

Conditions in steerage were not much improved, but the misery lasted a shorter time. ("Horrors of the Emigrant Ship." *Harper's Weekly*, 1869. Courtesy of The New-York Historical Society, New York City.)

Upon landing in New York, the early immigrants had to contend with the same kind of free-for-all that saw them off at Liverpool and other ports. The New York docks were crawling with swindlers and thieves. ("Landing from an Emigrant Ship." *Gleason's*, c. 1853. Courtesy of The New York Public Library Picture Collection.)

Between 1846 and 1925, some four million Irish would emigrate to the United States. ("Emigrants Leaving Queenstown for New York." *Harper's Weekly*, September 26, 1874. Courtesy of The New-York Historical Society, New York City.)

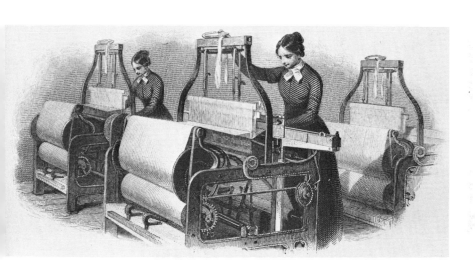

"There are several sorts of power working at the fabric of this Republic—water power, steam power, and Irish power. The last works hardest of all." (American Bank Note Co. "Lowell Girls." Engraving. Courtesy of the Prints Division, The New York Public Library.)

When the makeshift rooming houses had grown too full to cram in one more person, landlords built additional buildings in the yards behind them. ("Hell's Kitchen: Irish Neighborhood of Tenements." New York. Courtesy of the Museum of the City of New York.)

A Congressional inquiry in 1845 found that immigrants arriving in an election season were being naturalized about as soon as they stepped off the boat so that they could vote for Irish candidates. ("Naturalization of Foreigners in New York City." Wood engraving from Frank Leslie's *Illustrated News*, 1869. Courtesy of The New-York Historical Society, New York City.)

A draft list for the Union army in New York City in July 1863 included mostly Irish names. Tempers exploded, and a mob went on a rampage that lasted four days. "The Riots in New York: The Mob Burning the Provost Marshal's Office." *Illustrated London News,* August 1863. Courtesy of The New-York Historical Society, New York City.)

he rise of the Irish in urban politics was swift and thorough. By the end of the ivil War, Tammany was completely under Irish control. ("Tammany Hall, 1830." ithograph. *Valentine's Manual.* Courtesy of the Museum of the City of New York.)

/ the end of the nineteenth century, the United States was a manufacturing nation. orking-class Americans feared that "cheap Irish labor" would put them out of work bring wages down. (New England Factory Life. "Bell Time" by Winslow Homer. oodcut from *Harper's Weekly,* 1868. Courtesy of The New-York Historical Society, ew York City.)

As long as Catholics had been an unobtrusive minority, they did not threaten th
American way of life. But Irish Catholics were not inconspicuous. They changed th
character of city life in the East. (St. Patrick's Day in America. Parade in Unio
Square, early 1870s. Chromo-lithograph. Courtesy of the J. Clarence Davies Colle
tion, Museum of the City of New York.)

It took much longer for the Irish to capture the non-Irish vote. Alfred E. Smith was the first Irish-American to run for the presidency of the U.S. He lost to Herbert Hoover in 1928. (Laying the cornerstone of the new Tammany building in 1929. *Front row, left to right:* Willis Holly; James J. Walker, Mayor of New York; John R. Voorhis; and Alfred E. Smith. Courtesy of the Museum of the City of New York.)

With the passage of time, the Irish no longer seemed so "foreign," and another Catholic Irish-American, John F. Kennedy, set his sights on the presidency and was elected. (JFK being sworn in as president, January 1961. Courtesy of the John F. Kennedy Library.)

Chapter 9

"No Irish Need Apply"

John Doyle, an Irish immigrant who came to America in 1817, spent his first three months in Philadelphia working as a printer and in New York selling maps for a bookseller. He had saved his money and bought a stock of pictures, which he was now selling as a self-employed businessman. In January 1818 Doyle wrote to his wife in Ireland:

> I am doing astonishingly well, thanks be to God, and was able on the 16th of this month to make a deposit of 100 dollars in the bank of the United States.
>
> . . . [Here] a man is allowed to thrive and flourish without having a penny taken out of his pocket by government; no visits from tax gatherers, constables, or soldiers; everyone at liberty to act and speak as he likes, provided he does not hurt another; to slander and damn government, [and] abuse public men in their

office to their faces. . . . Hundreds go unpun-
ished for crimes for which they would be surely
hung in Ireland; in fact, they are so tender of
life in this country, that a person should have
[great difficulty] to get himself hanged for anything.[1]

Doyle's enthusiasm for America echoed that of
many other British immigrants who discovered prosperity and liberty in the New World.

But the path from Irish poverty to American
prosperity was not as short and straight for most
of the Irish immigrants who came in the 1840s.
Most Irish tended to stay in the cities, rather than
taking to the land. Many Irish-American leaders
tried to persuade their fellow countrymen to move,
as in the following 1855 editorial from *The Citizen*,
an influential Irish-American newspaper:

Westward Ho! The great mistake that emigrants, particularly Irish emigrants, make, on
arriving in this country is, that they remain in
New York, and other Atlantic cities, till they
are ruined, instead of proceeding at once to the
Western country, where a virgin soil, teeming
with plenty, invites them to its bosom. Here
. . . they become the easy prey of runners,
boarding-house keepers and other swindlers;
and, when their last cent is gone, they are
thrown into the street, to beg or starve or steal,
for employment there is none. Many, who in
their native land were strangers to drunkenness
and other vices, are here seduced by acts of the

villains by whom they are surrounded. . . .
Had they continued their journey westward,
without halting, many of them would be now
enjoying the happiness of independence. . . .
Their children and their children's children
would revel in the glories and grandeurs of
nature. . . .

What then is the duty of the unemployed or
badly paid emigrants residing in New York,
Philadelphia and Boston? To start at once for
the West.[2]

It would seem logical that people who had been
passionately attached to the land in Ireland would
take up a farming life here. But Thomas D'Arcy
McGee, an immigrant who became editor of *The
Boston Pilot*, commented on the irony of the Irish
becoming urban instead.

It has been a very strange accident that a
people who in Ireland hungered and thirsted
for land, who struggled for conacre [a land-
leasing contract in Ireland] and cabin even to
the shedding of blood, when they reached the
New World, in which a day's wages would have
purchased an acre of wild land in fee, willfully
concurred . . . to sink into the condition of a
miserable town tenantry, to whose squalor even
European sea ports would hardly present a
parallel.[3]

What kept most of the Irish in the cities? For one
thing, plowing, sowing, and harvesting large

acreages in America was different from planting and gathering potatoes on a small strip of land in Ireland. Also, farmers on the American frontier lived in isolation in untamed regions. In Ireland neighbors had lived nearby in a close-knit community. One Irishman who had gone west to prosper on a farm in Missouri looked back nostalgically to the fellowship he had enjoyed in Ireland:

> I could then go to a fair, a wake or a dance, or I would spend the winter nights in a neighbor's house, cracking the jokes by the turf fire. If I had there but a sore head I would have a neighbor within every hundred yards of me that would run to see me. But here everyone can get so much land, that they calls them neighbors that lives two or three miles off. . . . And [when I think of these things] then I would sit down and cry and curse him who made me leave home.[4]

The Irish also rejected the land, in part, because they no longer trusted it. It had been a harsh master, and had let them down too often. But the most important factor that kept many Irish from taking up land in the west was their poverty. Though land was free or cheap, it cost money for livestock, tools, and other supplies. Arriving penniless, the immigrants had to get jobs as quickly as possible, jobs at the bottom of the labor ladder.

And so, like the Chinese in the West, the Irish became the anonymous hands and backs of the East. A rapidly industrializing nation needed to get its work done. The Irish built the roads, canals, and railroads that crisscrossed the country. They built the cities' streets, houses, and sewer systems. This was grinding, dirty work with no future but more of the same. One newspaper described the Irish laborer's role in the growth of America in the 1850s:

> America demands for her development an inexhaustible fund of physical energy, and Ireland supplies the most part of it. There are several sorts of power working at the fabric of this Republic—waterpower, steam-power, and Irish-power. The last works hardest of all.[5]

Irish workers were paid poorly, and their work was hard and dangerous. It was not unusual for the father of a family to be dead by the age of forty. He would have died of an injury at work or of disease, which rampaged through the shantytowns and slums where the Irish lived. After reading an account, in 1836, of an Irish worker's accidental death, another Irishman said:

> How often do we see such paragraphs in the paper as an Irishman drowned—an Irishman crushed by a beam—an Irishman suffocated in a pit—an Irishman blown to atoms by a steam engine—ten, twenty Irishmen buried alive by the sinking of a bank—and other like casualties and perils to which honest Pat is constantly exposed in the hard toils for his daily bread.[6]

From 1840 Irish laborers laid most of the thirty thousand miles of railroad track that reached

Chicago from New York by 1856 and went on to St. Louis by 1860. These excerpts from "Pat Works on the Railway," a song of the time, tells their story:

> In eighteen hundred and forty-two
> I left the Old World for the New.
> Bad cess to the luck that brought me through
> To work upon the railway.
>
> In eighteen hundred and forty-three
> 'Twas then that I met sweet Molly McGee.
> An elegant wife she's been to me
> While working on the railway.
>
> In eighteen hundred and forty-four
> I traveled the land from shore to shore,
> I traveled the land from shore to shore
> To work upon the railway.
>
> In eighteen hundred and forty-five
> I found myself more dead than alive.
> I found myself more dead than alive
> From working on the railway.
>
> It's "Pat do this" and "Pat do that,"
> Without a stocking or cravat,
> Nothing but an old straw hat
> While I worked on the railway.
>
> In eighteen hundred and forty-seven
> Sweet Biddy McGee she went to heaven;
> If she left one kid she left eleven,
> To work upon the railway.[7]

The jauntiness of the song does not hide the suffering Irish workers and their families endured.

An immigrant who had worked the railroad gangs for twelve years let his bitterness boil over in a letter to Ireland in 1860:

> It would take more than a mere letter to tell you the despicable, humiliating, slavish life of an Irish laborer on a railroad in the States; I believe I can come very near it by saying that everything, good and bad, black and white, is against him; no love for him—no protection in life; can be shot down, run through, kicked, cuffed, spat on; and no redress, but a response of, "Served the damn son of an Irish b—— right, damn him."[8]

Anti-Irish feeling had grown rampant as the nineteenth century progressed and Irish immigrants poured into the country. Many employers refused to hire them. This prejudice was largely antiforeigner and anti-Catholic in nature. Many Americans feared the changes that might take place in their country because there were so many new ways arriving all at once from a people long held in contempt by the British. The middle- and upper-class Americans—once immigrants themselves—regarded the poverty in which the Irish lived—through no desire of their own—as a sign of inferiority. Working-class Americans feared that "cheap Irish labor" would put them out of work or bring wages down. These reasons for despising immigrants have remained in American society no matter what group was involved.

So, despite a shortage of labor throughout the nineteenth century and the willingness of the Irish to work long and hard, many doors to employment were closed to Irish immigrants. Patrick Ford, founder and editor of the New York newspaper, *Irish World*, recalled his discouraging experiences when he first arrived in the 1840s:

> I travelled footsore day after day through Boston for a place at a dollar a week, or at any price. I would see a notice, "Boy Wanted, No Irish Need Apply."[9]

Newspaper advertisements like these were common:

> CARPENTER—Skilled or unskilled for furniture shop. No Irish need apply.[10]

> WANTED. A Cook or a Chambermaid. They must be American, Scotch, Swiss, or Africans —no Irish.[11]

For many years, until the Irish in America developed some political and economic muscle, there was no way to fight the sign, No Irish Need Apply. Irish applicants simply had to look elsewhere for employment, but there was little elsewhere. Resentment at this injustice often resulted in brawling or verbal assault, as in the popular Irish-American song, "No Irish Need Apply":

> I'm a decent boy just landed from the
>   town of Ballyfad;
> I want a situation and I want it very bad.
> I've seen employment advertised. "It's just
>   the thing," says I,

But the dirty spalpeen [rascal] ended with
"No Irish Need Apply."
"Whoo," says I, "that is an insult, but to
get the place I'll try."
So I went there to see the blackguard with
his "No Irish Need Apply."

Chorus:
Some do think it is a misfortune to be
christened Pat or Dan,
But to me it is an honor to be born an
Irishman.[12]

I started out to find the house, I got there
mighty soon;
I found the old chap seated—he was
reading the *Tribune*.
I told him what I came for, when he in a
rage did fly;
"No!" he says. "You are a Paddy, and no
Irish need apply."
Then I gets my dander rising, and I'd like
to black his eye
For to tell an Irish gentleman "No Irish
Need Apply."

I couldn't stand it longer so a-hold of him
I took,
And I gave him such a welting as he'd get
at Donnybrook.
He hollered "Milia Murther," and to get
away did try,

> And swore he'd never write again "No
>   Irish Need Apply."
> Well, he made a big apology; I told him
>   then goodbye,
> Saying, "When next you want a beating,
>   write 'No Irish Need Apply.' "

The sign was not always out, however. Many Irishwomen found domestic work in private homes and in hotels, where Irish "girls" cleaned, cooked, ironed clothing, and made the beds. More often than not, these women would turn over their wages to their families here, or save their earnings to bring over brothers, sisters, and other relatives from "the other side." The McNabb family story is much like those of many other Irish of the time. Ann McNabb, a cook from a village near Londonderry, reported that her sister

> Maria—she was one of the twins—... died the famine year of the typhus. . . .
>
> Mother said when Maria died, "There's a curse on old green Ireland and we'll get out of it." So we worked and saved for four years ... and we sent Tilly to America. . . . She came to Philadelphia and got a place for general housework at Mrs. Bent's. Tilly got but two dollars a week, being a greenhorn. . . . She had no expenses and laid by money enough to bring me out before the year was gone. I sailed from Londonderry. . . . The passage was $12.

At first, her sister Tilly's employer took Ann on as a servant. Then Ann moved on to find her own niche.

> I got a place for general housework with Mrs. Carr. I got $2 till I learned to cook good, then $3 and then $4. I was in that house as cook and nurse for twenty-two years. Tilly lived with the Bents till she died, eighteen years. . . .
>
> Me and Tilly saved till we brought Joseph and Phil over, and they went into Mr. Bent's mills as weaver and spool boy, and then they saved and we all brought out my mother and father. We rented a little house in Kensington for them. There was a parlor in it and a kitchen and two bedrooms and bathroom and marble door step, and a bell. That was in '66, and we paid nine dollars a month rent. . . . It took all our savings to furnish it, but Mrs. Bent and Mrs. Carr gave us lots of things to go in. To think of mother having a parlor and marble steps and a bell!

The mother took in boarders at her Kensington house. Later, Ann's brother Joseph started a flour store, and Phil went to night school, married a schoolteacher, and started his career, in a prestigious manner for an Irish immigrant, as a clerk. The sisters continued to save and each finally owned her own house. Through self-denial and hard work the family survived, and the next generation was brought up in a manner more than an ocean apart from Ann McNabb's early years in Ireland:

Joseph did well in his flour store. He has a big one on Market Street now and lives in a pretty house out in West Philadelphia. He's one of the wardens in his church out there and his girls give teas and go to reading clubs.

But Phil is the one to go ahead! His daughter Ann—she was named for me but calls herself Antoinette—is engaged to a young lawyer in New York. He gave her a diamond ring the other day. And his son, young Phil, is in politics and a member of councils. He makes money hand over hand. He has an automobile and a fur coat, and you see his name at big dinners and him making speeches. . . .

It was Phil that coaxed me to give up work at Mrs. Carr's and to open my house for boarders here in Kensington. His wife didn't like to hear it said I was working in somebody's kitchen. I've done well with the boarders. I know just how to feed them so as to lay by a little sum every year. I heard that young Phil told some of his friends that he had a queer old aunt up in Kensington who played poor, but had a great store of money hoarded away. He shouldn't have told a story like that! . . . Last Sunday's paper had his picture and one of the young Lady he is going to marry in New York. It called him the young millionaire McNabb. But I judge he's not that. He wanted to borrow the money I have laid by in the old bank at Walnut and Seventh the other day and said he'd double it in a week. No such work as that for me! But the boy certainly is a credit to his family![13]

The McNabbs were not typical in the speed with which they rose to the middle class. But they were typical in their strong family ties and in the sacrifices they made to bring the family to the United States. Sometimes the sacrifices placed lives in peril. An Irish member of Parliament who visited the United States shortly after the Civil War told of a poor laborer who

emigrated to America in 1861, in the hope of bettering his condition, and . . . by hard work, to bring out his wife and seven children whom he had been compelled to leave after him in Ireland. It was an unpropitious time for a working man, as the war had just broken out, and employment was scarce in many cities of the Union. . . . [An] opportunity did offer rather unexpectedly, and in this way—a gentleman who preferred the profits of a lucrative business to the risks of war, desired to obtain a substitute, who would take his place for three years under the banner of the Union; and to secure someone to fight, or possibly, die, in his place, he was willing to pay down One Thousand Dollars. The poor Irishman heard of this dazzling offer, and at once accepted it. . . . He placed [the money] in the hands of a friend, directing him to send part to Ireland, to bring out his family, and reserve the balance to meet their wants on arrival—saying, if he

was killed in battle, or if he died of sickness, he
had done the best thing he could for his wife
and children.[14]

The soldier survived, but there were many who
didn't.

In spite of their low earnings the Irish in America
sent back astounding amounts of money to Ireland
to bring over others or to ease their families' lives
there. One million dollars a year went back in the
1840s. Over the next twenty years the figure rose to
ten million a year. Still, many Americans said the
Irish were wasteful spendthrifts.

However, other Americans opened their purses to
Ireland in the famine years. The citizens of Cincin-
nati contributed over $30,000 to Irish relief drives,
and New Yorkers raised over $200,000. The vice-
president of the United States, George M. Dallas,
led a national fund raising in 1847. It seems Americans found it easier to open their hearts to the Irish
"over there," then to help those who managed to
make their way over here. The immigrants were
considered a blight and a burden. They strained
municipal services, such as police and fire, health,
sanitation, and schools. Their presence meant higher
taxes because more support was needed for poor-
houses and other charitable institutions. There were
no welfare or social security programs at that time.

Then, as now, poverty in the cities bred drunkenness, crime, and despair. Americans blamed the
people rather than their circumstances for the sordid-
ness of their lives. They said the Irish were a dirty

race, slow-witted, given to drinking and fighting. An 1852 report of the New York Association for Improving the Condition of the Poor stated that Irish immigrants

> are but little disposed to change their thriftless habits with a change of country. Here, as in their own land, many of them evince too little force and energy to be arbiters of their own destiny. They are prone to stay where another race furnishes them with food, clothing, and labor. . . . Unlike immigrants of other nationalities, they have an utter distaste for felling forests, and turning up prairies for themselves; hence, they are mostly found loitering in cities and villages, and on the lines of our public works. . . . So pauperized in spirit and inefficient is the great mass in question, to say nothing of the ignorance, and physical and mental imbecility of many of them, that they cannot be made profitable laborers even in our Almshouses.[15]

Other Americans exploited the Irish and made profits from their misery. Landlords converted old residences and vacant warehouses into rooming houses, where each room housed an entire family. A Dr. Monnell, who served as a New York City sanitary inspector in the 1860s, recorded the conditions he saw:

> Passing from apartment to apartment, until we reached the upper garret, we found every place

crowded with occupants—one room, only 5½ by 9 feet, and a low ceiling, containing two adults and a daughter of twelve years, and the father working as a shoemaker in the room; while in the upper garret were found a couple of dark rooms kept by haggard crones, who nightly supplied lodging to twenty or thirty vagabonds and homeless persons.[16]

According to an 1845 New York City government report:

The most offensive of all places of residence are the cellars. . . . You must descend to them; you must feel the blast of foul air as it meets your face on opening the door; you must grope in the dark or hesitate until your eye becomes accustomed to the gloomy place, to enable you to find your way through the entry over the broken floor . . . you must inhale the suffocating vapor . . . and in the dark, dim recesses endeavor to find the inmates by the sound of their voices, or chance to see their figures moving between you and the flickering light of a window, coated with dirt and festooned with cobwebs.[17]

Dr. Pulling, another New York sanitary inspector, described a family:

The father of the family, a day laborer, is absent; the mother, a wrinkled crone at thirty, sits rocking in her arms an infant, whose pasty and pallid features tell that decay and death are usurping the place of health and life. Two older children are in the street, which is their only playground. . . . A fourth child, emaciated to a skeleton, and with that ghastly and unearthly look which marasmus [progressive emaciation caused by malnutrition] impresses upon its victims, has reared its feeble frame on a rickety chair against a window sill. . . . Its youth has battled nobly against the terribly morbid and devitalizing agents which have depressed its childish life—the poisonous air, the darkness, and the damp; but the battle is nearly over—it is easy to decide where the victory will be.[18]

Twenty years later things were much the same. The commissioners of the New York Board of Health reported in 1866 that nearly one third of the city's infants died in their first year. "The cause will best be sought in the miserable housing and habits of the laboring classes."

When the makeshift rooming houses had grown too full to cram in one more person, landlords built additional dwellings in the yards behind them. These rear tenements were dark, airless, and flimsy. Yet as fast as these instant slums were built, they were occupied at rents that made them among the most profitable real estate investment in the cities. Another New York sanitary inspector, Dr. Furman, reported that the tenements

are in many instances owned by large capitalists by whom they are farmed out to a class of

factors, who make this their especial business.
These men pay to the owner of the property a
sum which is considered a fair return on the
capital invested, and rely for their profits
(which are often enormous) on the additional
amount which they can extort from the
wretched tenants whose homes frequently become untenantable for want of repairs. . . .
These men contrive to absorb most of the
scanty surplus which remains to the tenants
after paying for their miserable food, shelter,
and raiment. They are, in many instances,
proprietors of low groceries, liquor stores, and
"policy shops" connected with such premises.
. . . Many of the wretched population are held
by these men in a state of abject dependence
and vassalage little short of actual slavery.[19]

"Groggeries" and "dramshops"—liquor stores and
taverns—abounded in the immigrant neighborhoods. Sober Protestants regarded Irish drinking as
proof of Irish moral inferiority. But the New York
commissioners of health said they knew from what
they had seen

and from the testimony of dispensary physicians
and other visitors among the poor, that the
crowded, dark, and unventilated homes . . .
[drive the immigrants] to habits of tippling. . . .
Pertinent was the reply of a drunken mother,
in a dismal rear-court, to a sanitary officer,
who asked her why she drank: "If you lived

in this place, you would ask for whisky instead of milk."[20]

Living conditions like these took their toll on the health of all the citizens. In the early nineteenth century, American cities had been generally healthy places compared to the cities of Europe. In Boston, for example, smallpox had almost been eliminated; there had been no major outbreak since 1792. After 1845 smallpox returned in epidemic proportions, particularly among the Irish. In 1849 cholera raged through Philadelphia, New York, and Boston. Tuberculosis, which had been declining in American cities, revived and flourished in the Irish slums, which became known as "fever nests."

A pioneer in public health systems, Dr. John Griscom, concluded in an 1845 report:

> The tide of emigration which now sets so strongly toward our shores cannot be turned back. We *must* receive the poor, the ignorant, and the oppressed from other lands. . . . No one, I presume, seriously believes they come with bad intentions, and then whose fault is it that they live here in cellars more filthy than the cabins of whose wretchedness we hear so much. . . .
>
> *We are parties to their degradation, inasmuch as we permit the inhabitation of places from which it is not possible that improvements in condition or habits can come.* . . . They are allowed, may it not be said required, to live in dirt. . . .

All society regulates the conduct of its members. . . . The "outcasts of society," constituting a very numerous tribe, form societies of their own, and stamp, in a degree, the character of the community of which they are a part. We have, as have all large cities, numbers of them with us, but they should be regarded not as such by choice, so much as by *compulsion*— as the creatures of circumstances beyond their control.[21]

But all the reports, commissions, and good intentions went unheeded. Even worse, in the decade after the 1845 report, the dislike and resentment of immigrants, particularly those who were Catholic, became the basis for a national political movement.

Chapter 10

America for Americans

When things change too quickly, people often grow angry or fearful. When they are faced by complex problems and have no immediate answers, they look for and often find other people—scapegoats—to blame for their troubles. In the years between the Revolution and the Civil War, American life changed a great deal. Cities grew bigger and dirtier, factories were drawing people away from farming, and many voices were demanding the vote for women and freedom for slaves. Immigrants were obvious and easy targets during these tense times.

The British Colonies were unique among the various colonial empires of the seventeenth and eighteenth centuries in freely accepting immigrants of almost any national or religious backgrounds. American colonists, from the very beginnings of European settlement, had mixed feelings about the differences among people coming to America. Though the doors remained open to immigrants after Independence, Americans retained a suspicion of strangers whose language, religion, and way of life were different.

One of the longest-lived and most strongly felt prejudices was against Catholics. The Puritans had left their homeland because they thought the seventeenth-century Church of England was "too Catholic" in its rituals and hierarchy. Even the less rigid Protestants carried a hatred of Catholicism with them to the New World. The most tolerant colony toward Catholics, Maryland, passed anti-Catholic laws along with the other colonies.

However, by 1830 religious passions had cooled. Nearly all the old laws restricting Catholics' civil rights had been done away with. The Catholic minority was small and discreet. Scholarly, cultured French clergy dominated the Church, which took on a somewhat aristocratic tone and stayed aloof from secular issues.

All of this changed with the "Irish invasion." The Irish were devoted to the Catholic Church. Poor and oppressed, the Church had worked with the Irish people against the English for reform and liberation. When all else failed, as it often did in Ireland, the Church provided comfort. The Irish wanted the Church to play a similar role in the United States, and the Church appointed more Irish priests and bishops to satisfy the large Irish congregations. In turn, the Irish clergy became active politically on issues affecting the education and welfare of their people.

As long as Catholics had been an unobtrusive minority, they did not threaten the American way of life. But Irish Catholics were not inconspicuous. Concentrated in the cities of the East, they changed the character of city life. The conspicuous Irish devotion to the Catholic Church awakened the suspicions of Protestants. Many Catholics, like Irish-born Bishop John Hughes, believed that since Catholicism was the true faith, the Church had an obligation to convert the rest of society. No one likes to be told his religion is wrong, and Bishop Hughes antagonized many Americans.

Americans also worried about the growing political strength of the Irish. Some of their concerns were well-founded. The Naturalization Act of 1802 had rescinded the harsh measures passed in 1798 in which the residence requirement for citizenship had been lengthened from five to fourteen years; the five-year requirement was reinstated. This was to last even against the strong nativist agitation for stricter laws in the 1840s and 1850s. In addition, states like New York (in 1821) had begun to abolish the property and tax-payer qualifications for voting. So the masses of Irish poor in the cities began to have an important political voice; with their long tradition of political activity, they knew how to make their numbers heard. It was the one sure way of gaining a place in a society that was biased against them.

A congressional inquiry in 1845 found that immigrants arriving in an election season were being naturalized almost as soon as they stepped off the boat so that they could vote for Irish candidates. The Whig party charged that the Democrats had won the presidential election of 1844 because of Irish votes, many of which were illegal. Philip Hone, mayor of New York, wrote in his diary on December 17, 1835:

> These Irishmen, strangers among us, without a feeling of patriotism or affection in common with American citizens, decide the elections in New York. They make Presidents and Governors, and they send men to represent us in the councils of the nation, and what is worse than all, their importance in these matters is derived from the use which is made of them by political demagogues.[1]

To make matters worse, according to some, Catholics from Italy and France were coming to America, too. George Templeton Strong, an influential New York lawyer, made the following entry in his diary on November 6, 1838:

> It was enough to turn a man's stomach—to make a man abjure republicanism forever—to see the way they were naturalizing this morning at the Hall. Wretched, filthy, bestial-looking Italians and Irish . . . the very scum and dregs of human nature, filled the . . . office so completely that I was almost afraid of being poisoned by going in. A dirty Irishman is bad enough, but he's nothing comparable to a nasty French or Italian loafer.[2]

Labor struggles began to erupt into violence. The newspapers usually blamed the Irish, not the people who had wronged them.

> July 16, 1831—On the 29th and 30th . . . it was known that a contractor on the 3rd division of the Baltimore and Ohio railroad, about 25 miles from the city, had absconded, leaving his laborers unpaid, and that they (as too often happens in Ireland, the country which, in general, they had recently left), had taken the law into their own hands, were wantonly destroying the property of the company, because their employer had wronged them! They were between 200 and 300 strong, and, with pick axes, hammers and sledges, made a most furious attack on the rails, sills, and whatever else they could destroy.[3]

Accounts like the above fed the anti-Catholic and anti-Irish fire. Anger and resentment led to violence against the despised groups. In 1831 a mob burned down the Ursuline convent in Charlestown, Massachusetts. Of the eight men brought to trial, seven were acquitted; the eighth was pardoned later. When Catholic children in the Philadelphia public schools were given permission to read the Douay (Catholic) rather than the King James (Protestant) version of the Bible in daily prayers, anti-Catholic speakers addressed mass meetings and whipped up mobs to burn Catholic churches and riot through Catholic neighborhoods. A nun at a Catholic orphanage wrote a midnight letter to her superior on May 9, 1844:

> We are in the midst of frightful dangers; a great portion of our peaceful city is the scene of a dreadful riot and bloodshed. Two of our Churches [are] burned to the ground. . . . St. John's has been guarded since Monday night, and St. Mary's is now surrounded by a strong detachment of the Military. . . . The clergymen have left their dwellings, the Bishop his house, the priests and students have deserted the seminary, everyone seeking a night's lodging in the family of some friends. Three police officers now guard our asylum, and we know not what moment our dear little ones must be roused from their peaceful slumbers, to fly for their lives. . . .
>
> The commencement of the disturbance was chiefly this: Many of the citizens had assembled to adopt some resolutions with regard to political affairs, when some Irish Catholic insulted them and made such a noise that the Speaker could not be heard. One word brought on another until a battle ensued. The truth is, it is nothing but a party of Protestants leagued against the Catholics, under the name of Native Americans [against] the Irish.[4]

The "Native American," point of view, as it came to be known, reviled foreigners in general and Catholics in particular. Respectable and prominent men like Samuel F. B. Morse, the inventor of the telegraph, were its advocates. Morse charged that Catholics were conspiring to subvert American democracy in alliance with the despotic nations of Europe that were sending over priests and immigrant agents to infiltrate and undermine the United States.

> We have now to resist the momentous evil that threatens us from Foreign Conspiracy. . . . Innocent and guilty are brought over together. We must of necessity suspect them all. . . . Up! up! I beseech you. Awake! To your posts! Let the tocsin [an alarm bell] sound from Maine to Louisiana. Fly to protect the vulnerable places of your Constitution and Laws. Place your guards; you will need them, and quickly, too. —And first, shut your gates. Shut the open gates.[5]

Political groups formed to "shut the gates." The Native American party held a national convention in 1845 to draw up a "declaration of principles" and devise a plan to defend American institutions "against the encroachment of foreign influence." The declaration stated that

> the civil institutions of the United States of America have been seriously affected, and that they now stand in imminent peril from the rapid and enormous increase of the body of residents of foreign birth, imbued with foreign feelings, and of an ignorant and immoral character, who receive, under the present lax and unreasonable laws of naturalization, the elec-

tive franchise and the right of eligibility to political office. . . .

The mass of immigrants . . . has increased from the ratio of 1 in 40 to that of 1 in 7! A like advance in fifteen years will leave the natives of the soil a minority in their own land! Thirty years ago these strangers came by units and tens—now they swarm by thousands.[6]

In 1854 the most successful nativist party was formed. The American party became better known as the Know-Nothing party, because when asked about their political activities, its members would reply, "I know nothing." The constitution of the party stated that

a member . . . must be a native-born citizen; a Protestant, born of Protestant parents, reared under Protestant influence, and not united in marriage with a Roman Catholic. . . .

The object of this organisation shall be to resist the insidious policy of the Church of Rome, and other foreign influence against the institutions of our country, by placing in all offices . . . none but native-born Protestant citizens.[7]

Just one year later the Know-Nothings controlled six state governments. Know-Nothings took every state office and almost all of the seats in the legislature in Massachusetts, which had the nation's second-largest Irish-Catholic population. Encouraged by their success on the state level, the Know-

Nothings ran former President Millard Fillmore as their presidential candidate in 1856. Fillmore was defeated, and the Know-Nothing party fizzled out. It had succeeded for a while because it played upon some Americans' fears about foreigners. In the end, it failed because other Americans could accept and adjust to the immigrants. Abraham Lincoln spoke for many people finally when, in 1855, he answered a question about his feelings on know-nothingism:

> How can anyone who abhors the oppression of negroes, be in favor of degrading classes of white people? Our progress in degeneracy appears to me to be pretty rapid. As a nation, we began by declaring that "*all men are created equal.*" We now practically read it, "all men are created equal, *except negroes.*" When the Know-Nothings get control, it will read, "all men are created equal, *except negroes, and foreigners and catholics.*" When it comes to this I should prefer emigrating to some country where they make no pretense of loving liberty.[8]

But nativism left its scars upon the Irish community and influenced Irish attitudes toward the slavery issue. While English, Welsh, and Scottish immigrants generally opposed slavery, the Irish, by and large, did not. They feared freed blacks would compete for the jobs the Irish held at the bottom of the economic ladder. Most of all, the Irish, who were preoccupied with their own miserable condition, thought it hypocritical of Northerners to sympathize with blacks while ignoring the plight of the poor of the Northern cities. The Irish had seen that many abolitionists were also nativists. Many, too were Northern business leaders who had no slaves but who discriminated against Irish workers, kept their wages low, and resisted attempts by workers to form labor unions. Congressman Mike Walsh of New York had been born in Ireland. In an 1854 speech in the House of Representatives he said:

> The only difference between the negro slave of the South and the white wage slave of the North is that the one has a master without asking for him, and the other has to beg for the privilege of becoming a slave. . . . The one is the slave of an individual; the other is the slave of an inexorable class.[9]

Nevertheless, when the Civil War began, the Irish rallied to the Union cause along with other British immigrants. Immigrants were grateful for the refuge and opportunities they had found in the United States. A Union soldier, Titus Cranshaw, wrote to his father in England:

> [There is not] as glorious a thing as keeping the Union safe and sound and not letting any portion of the United States turn to anarchy.[10]

However, British immigrants who had settled in the South, supported the Confederacy.

As the casualties mounted, Irish enthusiasm began to turn sour. In the North the law allowed a person who had been drafted to hire a substitute for three hundred dollars. Most Irish could not afford that sum and had to serve when called. Some Irishmen (like the poor laborer in the previous chapter) hired themselves out as substitutes for others in order to get money for their families. Resentment grew, and turned to violence in the summer of 1863.

A new draft list for New York City was drawn up in July. Most of the draftees were Irish. A crowd of disgruntled Irishmen gathered near the draft center. When the police tried to break up the crowd, tempers exploded, and the mob went on a rampage that lasted for four days. The rioters began by invading the draft offices. When soldiers were sent to restore order, the mob counterattacked; soldiers were beaten and a few were killed. Then:

> Having stopped the draft in two districts, sacked and set on fire nearly a score of houses, and half killed as many men, [the mob] now, impelled by a strange logic, sought to destroy the Colored Orphan Asylum on Fifth Avenue. . . . There would have been no draft but for the war—there would have been no war but for slavery. But the slaves were black, ergo, all blacks are responsible for the war. This seemed to be the logic of the mob. . . . Around this building the rioters gathered with loud cries and oaths, sending terror into the hearts of the inmates. Superintendent William E. Davis . . . with others, collected hastily the terrified children, and carrying some in their arms, and leading others, hurried them in a confused crowd out at the rear of the building, just as

the ruffians effected an entrance in front. Then the work of pillage commenced, and everything carried off that could be, even to the dresses and trinkets of the children, while heavy furniture was smashed and chopped up in the blind desire of destruction.

Colonel O'Brien, of the 11th New York Volunteers, had ordered his troops to fire into the mob. Later that day an angry crowd attacked him.

Knocked down and terribly mangled, he was dragged with savage brutality over the rough pavement, and swung from side to side like a billet of wood, till the large, powerful body was a mass of gore, and the face beaten to a pumice. . . .

The whole afternoon was spent in this fiendish work, and no attempt was made to rescue him. Towards sundown the body was dragged into his own back-yard, his regimentals all torn from him, except his pantaloons, leaving the naked body, from the waist up, a mass of mangled flesh clotted with blood.[11]

The draft riots were a shameful episode in the history of the Irish in America. But even as most Americans condemned the Irish for the rampage, they were also aware that Irish and other immigrants were fighting and dying in the war and that helped reduce some of the lingering nativist prejudice. Anti-foreigner and anti-Catholic feelings were not erased completely, however, and in years to come would be directed at new immigrant groups from southern and eastern Europe. But in fighting side by side with native-born Americans through four terrible years of civil war, Irishmen and other British immigrants earned their rights to be regarded and trusted as Americans.

Chapter 11

Leaders of Labor

The industrialization of America began early in the nineteenth century. During the Civil War soldiers wore factory-made, government-issue boots and uniforms. Once they became civilians, they were quick to accept mass-produced clothing, watches, furniture, hats, and soap. The population grew, and the demand for consumer goods grew with it. This, in turn, stimulated the steel and coal industries, which produced and powered the machines to make the goods and the railroads to carry them to consumers. By the end of the nineteenth century, the United States was a manufacturing nation.

English and Scottish workers left the factories and mines of their native lands to come to the United States in search of better industrial jobs in the 1830s and 1840s. They worked in the textile mills of New England, the factories of New York and Philadelphia, the mines of Pennsylvania, Ohio, and

Illinois. They soon learned the evils of industrial life in the United States.

A long and bitter struggle began as the workers joined forces to improve their situation. Robert MacFarlane, a Scottish dyer, organized a working-men's association in New York State in the 1840s. He expressed the views of many British immigrant workers when he said:

> The factory system has been long rooting out the Anglo-Saxon energy of England. . . . In our country, the evil is but faintly discerned because we are young in manufactures, but, Oh! I have seen enough of it to convince me of its future evils.[1]

The "future evils" had already come to pass and lasted a long time. Wages barely supported survival; working days were as long as twelve or fourteen hours; working conditions were unsafe and unsanitary. The owners and managers of industry had absolute power. As the workers were divided among themselves—men opposing women and children in industry, natives looking down on immigrants, whites refusing to work with blacks—exploitation was made all the more simple. Even at the turn of the century, the Irish-born labor organizer, Mother Jones, found conditions intolerable in the southern factory where she worked.

> This factory was run also by child labor. Here, too, were the children running up and down

between the spindles. The lint was heavy in the room. The machinery needed constant cleaning. The tiny, slender bodies of the little children crawled in and about under dangerous machinery, oiling and cleaning. Often their hands were crushed. A finger was snapped off.

A father of two little girls worked a loom next to the one assigned to me.

"How old are the little girls?" I asked him.

"One is six years and ten days," he said, pointing to a little girl, stoop shouldered and thin chested who was threading warp, "and that one," he pointed to a pair of thin legs like twigs, sticking out from under a rack of spindles, "that one is seven and three months."

"How long do they work?"

"From six in the evening till six come morning."

"How much do they get?"

"Ten cents a night."

"And you?"

"I get forty."

. . . They die of pneumonia, these little ones, of bronchitis and consumption. But the birth rate like the dividends is large and another little hand is ready to tie the snapped threads when a child worker dies.[2]

Most industrial workers, except in the New England states, were immigrants. Immigrants needed work desperately, and they had few skills to sell. Their labor was cheap. If workers protested and went on strike to improve the conditions of their work, there were always more immigrants arriving to replace them. And employers used unemployed immigrants as strikebreakers. The *New York Weekly Tribune* reported in 1846:

> As we understand it, a large number of Irish laborers have been at work in Winter for certain contractors for sixty-five cents per day, and the days were made pretty long at that. . . . As the rent of any decent tenement in Brooklyn would absorb nearly the entire earnings of a laboring man at this rate, they were allowed to build miserable shanties on ground allotted them by the contractors on the plot occupied by them in performing the work.
>
> . . . The poor laborers began to grumble at their hard lot, and at last united in an effort to improve it. They asked for 87½ cents per day and to have ten hours recognized as the limit of a day's work. The contractors refused to comply with their demands; whereupon the laborers struck work. The contractors hired a cargo of freshly landed Germans to take their places, and ordered the old laborers to quit the premises, which they refused to do, and resorted to the lawless, unjustifiable step of endeavoring to drive the Germans from the work by intimidation and violence. Of course the Military were called out, the Irish overawed, the Germans protected in their work, and thus the matter stands.[3]

Life was even worse for the miners, but their struggle to organize was more effective. Until the 1890s the majority of coal miners came from the British Isles and had served their apprenticeships in the coal pits of England, Scotland, and Wales. By 1901, with a quarter million members, they formed the largest group among the trade unions that comprised the American Federation of Labor (AFL). The mining union leaders' tactics and dedication inspired workers in many industries.

Terence Powderly, the son of Irish immigrants and a machinist, heard John Siney speak in 1869 in Pennsylvania. Over a hundred miners, most of them British, had been suffocated or burned to death in a fire in the Avondale mine. According to Powderly's autobiography:

> Siney . . . was the first man I ever heard make a speech on the labor question. I was just a boy then, but as I looked at Siney standing on the desolate hillside at Avondale . . . and listened to his low earnest voice, I saw the travail of ages struggling for expression on his stern, pale face. I caught inspiration from his words and realized that there was something more to win through labor than dollars and cents for self. I realized that death, awful death such as lay around me at Avondale, was a call to the living to neglect no duty to fellow man. John Siney gave expression to a great thought at Avondale when he said, "You can do nothing to win these dead back to life, but you can help

me win fair treatment and justice for the living
men who risk health and life in daily toil." The
thought expressed in that far away time became
my thought.[4]

Later, Powderly went on to become a leader of the
secret national labor organization, the Knights of
Labor, which was founded in 1869. The Knights of
Labor believed that "all who toiled" for a living,
skilled and unskilled, women, and blacks (with the
exception of doctors, lawyers, bankers, and liquor
dealers), had common interests and could join forces
to improve working conditions. The organization
dropped its pledge of secrecy in 1882 and reached
its peak of influence in January 1886 after a successful series of strikes against the railroads. It grew to
seven hundred thousand members, attracted many of
the most dedicated labor advocates of the time, and
had a large Irish membership.

Mother Jones—Mary Harris Jones—was one of
the organization's most forceful spokespersons. Born
in Ireland in 1830, Jones came to the United States
as a child. In 1861 she married an iron molder and
unionist in Memphis, Tennessee; they had four children. But tragedy struck in 1867, when a yellow
fever epidemic swept Memphis. In her autobiography Mother Jones wrote:

> Its victims were mainly among the poor and
> the workers. The rich and the well-to-do fled
> the city. . . . The poor could not afford nurses.
> Across the street from me, ten persons lay
> dead from the plague. The dead surrounded us.

. . . One by one, my four little children sickened and died. I washed their little bodies and got them ready for burial. My husband caught the fever and died. . . .

I returned to Chicago and went again into the dressmaking business with a partner. . . . We worked for the aristocrats of Chicago, and I had ample opportunity to observe the luxury and extravagance of their lives. Often while sewing for the lords and barons who lived in magnificent houses on the Lake Shore Drive, I would look out of the plate glass windows and see the poor, shivering wretches, jobless and hungry, walking along the frozen lake front. The contrast of their condition with that of the tropical comfort of the people for whom I sewed was painful to me. My employers seemed neither to notice nor care. . . .

The Knights of Labor was the labor organization of those days. I used to spend my evenings at their meetings, listening to the splendid speakers. . . .

I became acquainted with the labor movement. I learned that in 1865, after the close of the Civil War, a group of men met in Louisville, Kentucky. They came from the North and from the South. . . . They decided the time had come to formulate a program to fight another brutal form of slavery—industrial slavery. Out of this decision had come the Knights of Labor.

. . . I became more and more engrossed in the labor struggle and I decided to take an active part in the efforts of the working people to better the conditions under which they worked and lived. I became a member of the Knights of Labor.[5]

Mother Jones devoted the rest of her life to the union struggle. The Knights of Labor, however, lost effectiveness as a labor organization as a result of the Haymarket Riot in Chicago in May 1886. Following a violent strike on May 3 at the McCormick Harvesting Works, a meeting at the Haymarket was called for the following evening by labor leaders to protest the killing of a striker by police. At the May 4 meeting, an unknown person threw a bomb, killing seven policemen and four workers and injuring many others. Hysteria and anger followed, and eight social revolutionaries were arrested. (Four were eventually executed.) Organized labor, though not officially involved the night of the Haymarket tragedy, suffered a setback in the movement for an eight-hour workday and other improvements. The public turned against labor because of its seeming connection with violence, and union members themselves lost enthusiasm for organization. The AFL would survive, but the Knights of Labor did not.

By the end of the century British and Irish workers had gained some strength in the trades that they practiced. Some of them were becoming supervisors and foremen. The Irish were moving up from the menial, unskilled jobs the immigrants of the 1830s and 1840s had been forced to take. Instead of seeking a reform of society along the broad lines pursued by the Knights of Labor, British and Irish workers began to join a new, more militant organization.

By 1896 the American Federation of Labor had become the most important trade union organization in the United States, and British and Irish workers formed a large proportion of the initial leadership and membership. It had been founded and led through its early years by a British immigrant, Samuel Gompers, a cigar maker from London and member of the International Cigar Maker's Union, one of the most effective trade unions of the time. The AFL was a loose affiliation of unions, each of which directed its efforts toward the concerns of its own members.

Most of the membership were workers of foreign birth, but the AFL excluded unskilled workers, women, and blacks, and its goals were narrow ones aimed at improving salaries and working conditions for its members only. By the end of World War I, it included only a small percentage of the total labor force and had made only minor gains for its members, who were thwarted by employers who used troops, the courts, and a variety of coercive techniques against them. Still, it earned its place as the outstanding spokesman for the American worker when, in 1914, it won the eight-hour day for its members. Most Americans, however, continued to mistrust unions and to consider them a threat to the American belief that true *man* could become master of his fate without help from anyone.

Chapter 12

The Taking of Tammany and Other Irish Adventures in American Politics

At first, immigrant votes—English, Welsh, Scottish —were not important in American politics. But by the 1830s the Irish vote changed the nature of political campaigning, as the Irish carved out a political identity for themselves, especially in the "machine" politics of the cities.

The Irish had brought with them from Ireland a tradition of political passion, if not political power. They had fought to repeal the Penal Code and to establish the civil rights of Irish Catholics. Settling in American cities, they lived in Irish communities and shared common concerns.

Politicians were quick to see that the Irish, with proper handling, would work and vote for the candidates they preferred. The Irish, in turn, were quick to see that politics could provide a way to rise in the world. Irish immigrants needed jobs and other assistance. Becoming a policeman, fireman, or city clerk was a giant step up in American society for immigrants who were unskilled laborers, whose children had to help support their families. As one newspaper noted:

> If politics are necessary to the existence of Irishmen, they can get plenty of the needful in this country. Our Celtic friends are good at voting, they vote early and sometimes often, and as a general thing can be relied upon for the whole Democratic ticket.[1]

The Irish immigrants who arrived before the Civil War were drawn to the Democratic party because the Democrats were (like their ideological forebears, the Jeffersonian Republicans), for the most part, friendly toward immigrants. The Federalists and the Whigs were not. The Democratic party identified itself with the aspirations of the "common man" against the opposition parties, which were more upper class. When Andrew Jackson ("Old Hickory") ran for his second term as President as the champion of the "common man," Irish support in New York helped carry the state for him in 1832.

In a letter to the editor of a New York newspaper following the 1832 presidential election a group of Irish workers defended their choice, which went hard on them.

> We the subscribers, natives of Ireland—and adopted citizens of the United States—have been in the employment of Hance and Brooks, carpenters, in the Sixth Ward for some time. . . .
> The above carpenters were active in the

cause of the opposition in the late election. . . . Mr. T. C. Colt, foreman to the above firm, presented to the subscribers a set of opposition tickets each, and said to us, if we would go to the polls and vote these tickets, that each one should receive his wages for any time lost on that occasion. . . . The above tickets were indignantly refused by every man, as well as the proffer of wages, and our reply was that we should go to the polls and vote according to our consciences, and any time spent there we were willing to lose; for we would vote for "Old Hickory"—the Man of the People!!

The conduct of the above employers was most materially altered towards us on the following morning . . . one of them . . . said that Irishmen should not be encouraged in this country, and that he would not have one of them about his premises—that he would sooner have inferior workmen, if any others could not be obtained, than have an Irishman employed in the future. The aforesaid Hance and Brooks . . . kept their word, for the next day they discharged from their employment every Irishman in the concern![2]

In spite of such setbacks, the rise of the Irish in urban politics was swift and thorough. For example, New York's Tammany Society, which became the most important Irish political stronghold in the country, was originally formed in 1789 by native-born Protestant workingmen with an antiimmigrant bias. For many years the Tammany leaders refused to nominate any Irish Catholic for public office. But heavy Irish immigration in the 1840s and 1850s and the power of the Irish vote forced Tammany to make concessions. By the end of the Civil War, Tammany was completely under Irish control.

Throughout the large cities of the Northeast and Midwest, the Irish painstakingly built Democratic machines—party organizations that control policy—which formed "shadow governments" of their own. The machines provided services for the Irish-American that the regular government either could not or would not provide. Social workers and reformers in the Irish slums of Boston described in a report published in 1899 how the shadow governments, or machines, worked.

> There are usually in the tenement-house sections several distinctly political clubs. Standing at the head of these is the "machine club." . . . All the men in the ward having good political jobs are members. In one local club it is estimated that the city employees belonging to it draw salaries to the amount of $30,000 per year. . . . It is natural that all the men in these clubs are anxious to maintain the machine. It is a question of bread and butter with them. . . .
>
> The boss has reduced to a science the knack of dominating men. . . . The frown of the boss is supposed to carry terror to the hearts of those to whom he has rendered favors or who expect jobs. This is easily accounted for, as without

his approval no one in the ward can get a city job.

On the whole, partly for the love of position and power, and partly from a good heart, the boss enjoys doing good turns for men. Stories are told by his admirers of his generous deeds. . . . At Christmastime and Thanksgiving he gives turkeys to certain needy families. Dance tickets, baseball passes, tickets to the theater, railway passes, and so forth . . . are distributed with wise discrimination. . . . This all sounds very generous; but . . . every man to whom he has granted a favor is made to feel that the boss expects a vote.[3]

"Getting out the vote" gave Irish machine politicians great power for many generations, and discrimination against the Irish pushed many Irish-American men of talent into this inviting future.

There is in these wards a considerable number of young men who regard politics as El Dorado. They are poor but ambitious. Many of them have received a fairly good education. It more and more requires a "friendly pull' in order to secure a good position in business. In business, too, they have to meet stong prejudices of race and religion. Politics, therefore, is for them apparently the easiest way to success in life. In every ward such as we are describing, there are a few conspicuous examples of men living in comfort, who are reported rich and have made their money in politics. It is told you, for instance, that the mother of one of these men lived in a garret and went barefoot out of sheer poverty. Thus the clever young fellow is encouraged to try his hand.[4]

To those who had little or no contact with immigrants in the cities—and this meant most Americans—the give-and-take style of machine politics seemed sinister. In 1866 the editor of *The Nation* magazine expressed the fears of many when he wrote:

> The purses of the rich cities are everywhere passing into the hands of the ignorant, the vicious, and the depraved, and are being used by them for the spread of political corruption. . . . When knaves have reached such a point of audacity as to sell regularly the teacherships in our public schools in order to provide funds for their own carousals, it is . . . time for us . . . to put an end to these abuses.
>
> We all know what the source of the evil is. In all our large towns a swarm of foreigners have alighted, ignorant, credulous, newly emancipated, brutalized by oppression, and bred in the habit of regarding the law as their enemy, the rich as their tyrants. . . .
>
> Foreigners now are no longer in the same relation with the American community which they were when they arrived at the rate of a few shiploads a year. They are not scattered through it, exposed at every turn to be acted upon by its opinion, habits, and manners. . . .

> They form, on the contrary, large, compact
> communities of their own, perfectly impervious
> to American influences, in which no Americans
> are ever seen except on business errands, in
> which American opinions are never heard,
> American papers never read . . . —commu-
> nities, in short, as distinctive, as essentially
> foreign, as the population as Dublin or Ham-
> burg, and kept constantly recruited by fresh
> arrivals.[5]

But for the immigrants, the machines gave government a human face at a time when the government did as little as possible for the lives of its
citizens in trouble. If a workman was injured on the
job, the machine might get some compensation for
him. If a member of an immigrant family was in
trouble with the law, the machine could often help.
If an immigrant was unemployed, the machine
would send coal and food to its family.

George Washington Plunkitt was a Tammany
politician for forty-five years. In a series of interviews in 1905, Plunkitt explained how the machine
worked to capture voters:

> What tells in holdin' your grip on your district
> is to go right down among the poor families
> and help them in the different ways they need
> help. I've got a regular system for this. If there's
> a fire in Ninth, Tenth, or Eleventh Avenue, for
> example, any hour of the day or night, I'm
> usually there with some of my election district
> captains as soon as the fire engines. If a family

is burned out, I don't ask whether they are Republicans or Democrats, and I don't refer them to the Charity Organization Society, which would investigate their case in a month or two and decide they were worthy of help about the time they are dead from starvation. I just get quarters for them, buy clothes for them . . . and fix them up till they get things runnin' again. It's philanthropy, but it's politics, too—mighty good politics. Who can tell how many votes one of these fires brings me? The poor are the most grateful people in the world. . . .

To those who complained about corruption and said the bosses got rich at public expense, Plunkitt said:

Everybody is talkin' these days about Tammany men growin' rich on graft, but nobody thinks of drawin' the distinction between honest graft and dishonest graft. There's all the difference in the world between the two. . . . I've made a big fortune out of the game, and I'm gettin' richer every day, but I've not gone in for dishonest graft—blackmailin' gamblers, saloonkeepers, disorderly people, etc.—and neither has any of the men who have made big fortunes in politics.

There's an honest graft, and I'm an example of how it works. I might sum up the whole thing by sayin': "I seen my opportunities and I took 'em."

Just let me explain by examples. My party's in power in the city, and it's goin' to undertake a lot of public improvements. Well, I'm tipped off, say, that they're going to lay out a new park at a certain place.

I see my opportunity and I take it. I go to that place and I buy up all the land I can in the neighborhood. Then the board of this or that makes its plans public, and there is a rush to get my land, which nobody cared particular for before.

Ain't it perfectly honest to charge a good price and make a profit on my investment and foresight? Of course, it is. Well, that's honest graft.

The Tammany sage praised what the Irish had done for politics, and what politics had done for the Irish.

One reason why the Irishman is more honest in politics than many Sons of the Revolution is that he is grateful to the country and the city that gave him protection and prosperity when he was driven by oppression from the Emerald Isle. . . .

Yes, the Irishman is grateful . His one thought is to serve the city which gave him a home. He has this thought even before he lands in New York, for his friends here often have a good place in one of the city departments picked out for him while he is still in the old country. Is it any wonder that he has a tender

spot in his heart for old New York when he is
on its salary list the mornin' after he lands?[6]

Irish politicians took virtual control of cities like
New York and Boston and were powerful in other
cities with large Irish populations, like Chicago and
Philadelphia. But it took much longer for them to
capture the non-Irish votes.

Alfred E. Smith was the first Irish-American to
run for the presidency of the United States. Smith
had served four terms as Democratic governor of
New York, and was one of the best governors in the
state's history. In 1928 Smith was the Democratic
candidate for President, but he lost the election to
Herbert Hoover, a Republican. Because Al Smith
was an urban Catholic of Irish descent, he was sus-
pect in many parts of the country, especially in the
South and rural areas of the Midwest. Although the
1928 election is still being analyzed, and many
historians believe that any Democrat would have lost
that year, Smith and many of his fellow Catholics
believed he would have won it had it not been for
his religion. Until that time no presidential candidate
had been asked to justify his religious views, but
during the campaign, Smith felt called upon to
defend his.

> In your open letter to me in the April *Atlantic
> Monthly*, you "impute" to American Catholics
> views which, if held by them, would leave
> open to question the loyalty and devotion to
> this country and its Constitution of more than
> 20 million American Catholic citizens. . . .

. . . You imply that there is conflict between religious loyalty to the Catholic faith and patriotic loyalty to the United States. Everything that has happened to me during my long public career leads me to know that no such thing is true. I have taken an oath of office in this state nineteen times. Each time I swore to maintain and defend the Constitution of the United States. . . . I have never known any conflict between my official duties and my religious belief. No such conflict could exist. Certainly the people of this state recognize no such conflict. They have testified to my devotion to public duty by electing me to the highest office within their gift four times.[7]

After Smith was defeated, the United States went through the Great Depression and World War II. With the passage of time the Irish no longer seemed so "foreign," especially as refugees fleeing the Nazis and later the Communists came to America from all parts of Europe.

Another Catholic Irish-American, John F. Kennedy, set his sights on the presidency. His genealogy reads like a capsule of the Irish experience up the American political ladder. His mother's father, John Fitzgerald, had been mayor of Boston. On Kennedy's father's side, his great-grandfather had been an immigrant, his grandfather a ward boss in East Boston. A Democratic President, Franklin D. Roosevelt, had appointed his father, Joseph P. Kennedy, ambassador to Great Britain in 1938, the first Irish-American and first Catholic to hold the post. But like Al Smith, John F. Kennedy felt compelled to explain his position. In a speech before the Greater Houston (Texas) Ministerial Association in September 1960, he said:

> Because I am a Catholic, and no Catholic has ever been elected President, the real issues in this campaign have been obscured. . . . So it is apparently necessary for me to state once again, not what kind of church I believe in, for that should be important only to me, but what kind of America I believe in.
>
> I believe in an America where the separation of church and state is absolute. . . .
>
> . . . I believe in an America where religious intolerance will someday end. . . .
>
> I believe in a President whose views on religion are his own private affair. . . .
>
> This is the kind of America I believe in— and this is the kind of America I fought for in the South Pacific and the kind my brother died for in Europe. No one suggested then that we might have a "divided loyalty," that we did "not believe in liberty" or that we belonged to a disloyal group that threatened "the freedoms for which our forefathers died."
>
> . . . Contrary to common newspaper usage, I am not the Catholic candidate for President. I am the Democratic Party's candidate for President who happens also to be a Catholic. I do not speak for my church on public

matters—and the church does not speak for me. . . .

. . . If this election is decided on the basis that 40 million Americans lost their chance of being President on the day they were baptized, then it is the whole nation that will be the loser in the eyes of Catholics and non-Catholics around the world, in the eyes of history, and in the eyes of our own people.[8]

By his election and his conduct in office, John Kennedy defused "the Catholic issue" in American national politics.

Chapter 13

The Road Goes Ever On: Conversations with Irish and Scottish Immigrants

Immigrants from the British Isles began coming to North America before the United States was born. During the nineteenth century, the first century of the new nation, British and Irish immigrants were the most numerous and prominent of the newcomers. In the second century their numbers were eclipsed by people coming from other parts of Europe, Asia, and Latin America. Yet from 1876 through the first quarter of the twentieth century, British and Irish immigrants and their descendants provided much of the drive and leadership in the movements that concerned immigrant workers and voters.

Although people continue to immigrate from the British Isles, the numbers are relatively small. The population of the United States is so large and diverse, and the economy so complex, that these recent immigrants are barely noticeable. Today, English, Scottish, and Irish immigrants feel at home

144

and fit in easily. Welsh immigration had virtually ended by the 1920s.

But British immigrants still experience variations on the themes that have run all through this history. The largest contingent of twentieth-century immigrants from the British Isles still comes from Ireland. Poverty is the main reason for emigration according to Bill MacDonald, who came in 1947. He recalled that during the World War II years in Ireland:

> I lived in a rural area. We had approximately 15 acres of land. There was six of us in the family. My father was a farmer.
>
> During the war, it was really terrible. It was probably even worse than in England. When we got home from school, we had a day's work to do on the farm. We used to have to go to the bog and cut our turf—our fuel for heating the house, for fires in the wintertime. I remember distinctly having a few bad seasons with very wet weather over there. We had to use every method possible to dry the turf, to make a fire and keep warm, while we were sometimes having two meals of potatoes a day. No meat, forget that! We used to get a small ration of sugar. And even today I don't take sugar in my tea because I remember giving the sugar up for my mother. You didn't have much as far as material things, but you had a relationship with the rest of your family like I don't think they enjoy at all in this country.

I imagine what would be responsible for it was we did have a lot of poverty, and it seems like love breeds in poverty. You live so much together. You just don't have any place to go, really. When it got dark and your jobs were finished for the day, you sat around the fire, and you talked or you played cards, or you listened to your grandfather tell old stories of revolutionary days.

I always used to admire people coming home from the United States when I was a kid—seeing how well-dressed they were, and all. They seemed to always have money—something we never could enjoy. I said, if it were possible when I grew up, this is what I'd like to do, if I couldn't get a job in Ireland. Come to the United States.

Many Irish still live poorly in Ireland, barely scratching out a living, unemployed, or on relief. In 1921, after seven centuries of English domination, an Irish nation was established, the Irish Free State, or Eire in Gaelic, now called the Republic of Ireland. It was a bloody birth; many Irish and English died in the conflicts that led to independence. And the price of independence was high as far as Irish patriots were concerned. The twenty-six counties that make up the Republic are the poorest and least developed of all the nations of northwestern Europe. Six other counties, of the province of Ulster, with large Protestant populations, were partitioned from the Catholic counties and remained part of Great Britain.

Die-hard Irish patriots refused to accept partition. They continued to wage war against the Irish government for leaving Ulster in English hands; but at last the Civil War ended in 1923 with the government forces in control and Ulster, or Northern Ireland, separated from the Republic. But that didn't signify the end of the conflict. The Provisional wing of the Irish Republican Army (IRA) went underground, and the "Provos" continue to wage the campaign to unite all Ireland to this day.

At the close of the Civil War, many of those who fought against the government found that lingering resentment against them made it hard to get by. Sean Lyons's account of the Civil War reflects his political feeling. Not all Irish would agree with his interpretation, but many do.

> I arrived in America on the fourteenth day of February, 1927—Valentine's Day. I came from County Tipperary, and I was 24 years old.
>
> We had just been through a civil war which arose over the treaty with England in 1921. The majority of the people did not like the treaty. The treaty did not give them full freedom. It gave them a sort of commonwealth status. So the people rejected it. However, the affluent people and the church—all denominations—were in favor of it. Then the treaty did another thing that was objectionable to almost all classes of people: that is, it divided Ireland.

They divided it on the grounds of bigotry, and another reason: that the largest shipbuilding yards in Europe at the time happened to be situated in Belfast.

Now there was a civil war fought in the South about this, against the government set up on the lines of the treaty. And after the Civil War, people like myself, who took part against the treaty, were ostracized. We had finally surrendered and were imprisoned. After our release from prison, we found that we were blackballed as far as jobs were concerned. So I saw no alternative but to get out of the country.

Until the 1960s most immigrants came over by ship. Though there were vast improvements from the time of the "famine ships," immigrants could still find the passage rough going, as Sean Lyons remembered:

It wasn't a pleasant trip. It took me 14 days, I think, to get here because there were tremendous storms at sea. I was very sick for several days.

The other passengers were mostly Irish. They were quite jolly, but I could see that there was quite a lot of lonesomeness about some of them, and they were singing songs to try and keep them from thinking about this lonesomeness of what they were facing.

Jim O'Neill, another IRA veteran who left Ireland in 1926, recalls a cheerier passage and the assistance given him by a countryman when he arrived in New York:

> It was a seven day trip at that time. It was pleasant, you know—a lot of young people. All the people who were leaving Ireland at that time were young. We had a nice time coming across.
>
> I landed in 14th Street. We hadn't much inspections of any kind. Of course, we hadn't much stuff either. Each of us had just one bag. We walked off the boat and came up on 9th Avenue. There was an elevated subway there at the time. We spoke to an old fellow there. He was a dock worker, so I figured he was Irish. I asked him directions, said we wanted to get to 116th Street. So the old-timer says to us, "Have you any American money?" I said, "No." So he says, "I'll give you four nickels. Each of you drop one in that slot that you'll see when you go up there," he said, directing us to the El. Sure enough, we went up the stairway and dropped in our nickels, and got into the train and got up to 116th Street. From there it was only a short walk to where my friend's family lived, and we went up to their apartment and that was it—we were in America.

Friends and family already here helped newcomers settle in and get jobs. They could be particularly helpful if they had political connections, as Jim O'Neill explained:

The first job I got was with the Consolidated Gas. My brother-in-law belonged to the Democratic Club, and he talked to the district leader and he was down the following Monday morning offering me a job.

Many Irish, though, did not have the way paved for them. They had hard times finding jobs because they were aliens. And the jobs they found were often unpleasant and poorly paid. This was how Bill Mac-Donald found it in 1947.

I was refused in several places before I finally secured a job. I was refused employment because I was an immigrant, not a citizen. I took a job that the average American wouldn't take. I was exploited. I didn't realize it then, but now I know that I was. My job was washing metal parts in all kinds of corrosive stuff like paint remover. My hands used to be raw from my elbows down, just bare flesh, to the point where I couldn't hardly sleep at night.

And then I took another job, too. I used to get out of work at 4:30, and then at 5:00 I'd go to work again as an usher in a theater. I made 50 cents an hour and all the popcorn you could eat. I'd get home at 12 o'clock at night, and then it would be the same routine the next day. The reason I took two jobs was that a brother of mine expressed interest in coming to the United States, and I wanted to get him out here.

English and Scots continued to come to America
as well as Irish. While living conditions weren't as
bad in Great Britain as they were in Ireland, there
were hard times, particularly in the less industrialized regions. The British economy dived into a depression after World War I, and dived deeper during
the worldwide slump of the 1930s. Many ambitious
and adventurous young people decided to try their
luck in the United States. Mary Darroch left Scotland on an impulse in 1928.

> I came in 1928—April. It was very nice at
> home. It wasn't that I was hard up. I was work-
> ing at the time in a carpentry business. I was a
> bookkeeper.
>
> A girlfriend of mine had come over here,
> and she was writing to me all about the fun and
> everything else, and I thought I'd like to come
> here, too. Why I decided that I don't know.
> Maybe it sounds silly, but I always say fate
> takes a hand in your life, and you do things.

Mary's boyfriend John Darroch, who became her
husband, followed her a year later.

> Mary left in 1928, and I got rather restless after
> that. So I came to America in February, 1929.
> Quite a lot of young people in our town left.
> Mary and I had been working, but at that time
> it was very bad. There was a depression in Scot-
> land, begun right after the war. And you
> always thought you could get something better
> here, in America. It's a so much bigger country.

Things were not easy at first. Mary, who had been a clerical worker in Scotland, had to take lower-level jobs here.

> I had to do housework when I first came. That's all the work there was. It was hard for me because I had never done housework in my life. The first place I worked in, they had two youngsters. And I never call children brats, but they were brats. And the lady of the house wanted me washing windows and cleaning everything all the time. So I came to visit my friends who had come to Brooklyn first. And I was crying. By that time I was homesick and wishing I was back there. But pride won't let you go back. So I was crying and telling my friend how they were so rotten to me. So my friend said, "Listen, you're not going back. I'll call that lady and tell her you're not coming back."

> So in those days you went to agencies after jobs. And I went. They sent me to a candy factory. And I was put to some kind of machine where you roll a string about a five-pound box of candy that would then go to the candy store.

> Factory workers—not that I have anything against factory workers—but they were some tough ones. They were different from what I was. The way some of them used curse words!

Even though the American language and American ways were not totally strange, immigrants from the British Isles inevitably experienced some culture shock. Bill MacDonald, the Irishman who came after World War II, had a rude shock when he encountered disparaging remarks about the Irish.

> I found that the American people could be very offensive by making little of things that we thought an awful lot about—sometimes our religious beliefs or family customs. It was commonplace. I guess it was brought over by the Anglo-Saxons, creating that inferior atmosphere about the Irish. People at the place where I worked constantly made references to Irish life, and the ignorant Irish "Mick" or "Pat." It was very hurtful.

> This was the thing that really amazed me in the factory where I worked. You'd go to the men's room for a break, and there would be several people in there. One would refer to the other as a Polack, and the other would refer to another guy as a Guinea. And, of course, the Black would be left out in the cold altogether. And I used to try to distinguish one from the other—the "Polack" from the "Guinea." I could never tell. It knocked me back a peg, and for a while I had second thoughts about this type of feeling. It was very disappointing that this type of thing could be tolerated in a country that you always looked at as the foundation of equal justice.

In the six counties of Ulster which have remained part of Great Britain, Catholics must compete fiercely with Protestants for an inadequate number of jobs and are often left out in the cold. Catholics who are employed often have to take the lowest-grade and lowest-paid jobs. Maureen O'Donnell, who emigrated from Northern Ireland in the late 1960s, told why she left in an interview:

In my own family, immigration to America started in the famine years. And the generations have been coming to this country ever since: the younger generation joining the last, and so on down the years. I would not be satisfied to join an unemployment line, to receive unemployment benefits from the British government and to remain unemployed for the rest of my life. And that was basically what I would face if I lived in Ireland. Of course, one could wash dishes for some local person, and barely exist on the money one would make. The better jobs, the government jobs, were just not available to the likes of myself who graduated from a Catholic high school.

It is hereditary to leave Ireland, you know. One doesn't stop to think. As you were closer to graduating from high school, you began to wonder what country you're going to, to find a job in. One could consider going to England or America. And one usually went to the country where one had relatives. As most Irish families have relatives in the U.S., so do I. My oldest sister had already come, left Ireland when she was seventeen. Two years later, she invited me to come along after I finished high school.

She recalled that when she arrived,

> I didn't even know American money. I had
> arrived in New York on a Thursday, and the
> next Monday I started to work. And at 11
> o'clock break when the coffee cart came
> through the office, I had money but I didn't
> know how to spend it. I just didn't know the
> value of it. Several people in that office took
> me under their care. And for months on end,
> each day they made sure they had somebody
> to travel with me to the subway, someone
> to go with me to the coffee shop for lunch. I just
> couldn't understand the kindness. I didn't think
> you had that sort of life in New York. There
> was great hospitality.

The American standard of living was also a sur-
prise. Ian Keown, Mary Darroch's nephew, came
from the same town in Scotland as his aunt, but
some thirty years later in 1960. He wasn't able to
land a job in his field, advertising, right away, so
Keown took a temporary job.

> When it was obvious that I wasn't going to get
> a job right off, I decided I'd better have some
> income coming in, so I applied for a job as a
> part-time salesman over Christmas at Macy's.
> The reason for choosing Macy's was that I had
> heard of it. It was the largest store in the world.
> And it seemed to me it would be a good op-
> portunity to get some ideas of the American
> economy.

I learned that the American economy was pretty powerful. There was an awful lot of money going through there, and people were spending an awful lot of money on what seemed to me very, very fringe items. I was working in a department called Gifts for Men, which included things like pewter beer steins, and ceramic steins, and hand-carved wooden galleons from Portugal which were selling for about 400 dollars in cash. Four hundred dollars! In Scotland, you buy socks and handkerchiefs for people's Christmas gifts. You don't buy 400 dollar gifts.

Ian Keown had come to the United States not because he was poor, but because opportunities in his field were better in the United States than in Britain. He became part of the movement known in the 1950s and 1960s as the brain drain. Working-class emigration had practically stopped with the establishment of a socialist economy in Britain after World War II. Workers had a strong voice in government to improve their lot, so despair no longer pushed them out of their country.

But the changes in the British economy meant other things to people in the business and professional classes, who began to leave in large numbers for the United States and Canada. Business people felt hampered by skyrocketing taxes and the demands of the British labor unions. Doctors were unhappy about the salaries paid by the National Health Service. Scientists came because there was more money to fund scientific research in the United States than in Britain. And the booming American economy of those years welcomed these gifted, highly educated British professionals.

Keown spoke about his brighter prospects:

> I was born in a town in Scotland called Greenock, which was an industrial town upon the river Clyde about 20 miles from Glasgow. I was educated there, and then afterwards decided that my interests were artistic, in writing. The most appropriate thing for me would be to be in advertising, I thought. And that determined the rest, because once you want to be in advertising, a place like Greenock is no good.
>
> You go to Glasgow, which is the biggest city in Scotland. There's a limited market for advertising there, so next I went to London. I lived in London for five years, working in various advertising agencies.
>
> Everyone in advertising sooner or later wants to come to New York. It's the big place. It's like if you're a priest, you want to go to Rome to study. Financially you do better here. The volume of advertising going through New York is so much greater than that going through London that they can afford to pay much higher salaries. I think the salaries in London are much more realistic. The salaries in advertising here are just outrageous. Because of the big budgets, though, New York is still the place to come if you're in advertising.

The fact that I was from overseas counted against me only in the sense that they really had no way of evaluating my background. Here, if you switch agencies, they pick up the telephone and they get an evaluation of you from the other people you worked for. But they had to take my word for it that everything I had put on my resume was, in fact, true. People were reluctant to hire a foreigner in a field like advertising where you don't have a specific degree as a doctor has. If you come over as a writer and say you can do anything, there's no guarantee that you can.

For her part, Maureen O'Donnell felt very much a stranger here at first.

One of the problems of coming to a new country was that of identity. If you've lived in an area for some time, then you've built up a certain amount of credibility. If you're a newcomer, whether you're going to an apartment building to get an apartment, or to the telephone company to get a telephone, or to the business world to get employment, you've got to build up your own identity, your own credibility. And that's one of the real difficulties. One doesn't have a family to identify with. You've got to be taken at face value. You've got to prove just by your own hard work that you are honest, you are truthful, you are willing to work.

Maureen O'Donnell, Bill MacDonald, and John and Mary Darroch, all came to the United States intending to stay. Ian Keown, Sean Lyons, and Jim O'Neill each came intending to stay just a few years and then return to Britain or Ireland. Yet they are still here, and all but Keown have become American citizens. Becoming naturalized is the final step in leaving the home country for good. Happy as a person might be in the United States, it is nevertheless a hard step for many an immigrant to take. John Darroch described how it felt to him.

> I became a citizen because of our son. I was hesitating about it a long time. But my son kept saying, "When are you going to become a citizen?" At election time, the teachers would say, "Of course, your parents vote." So we became citizens because our son was an American.
>
> Even though I left Scotland when I was very young, it gives you a funny feeling when you swear you'd not have anything to do with the country you were born in. It gives you goose pimples. You swear you'll have nothing more to do with your king and queen. And you swear allegiance to the flag of the United States of America. But I've never regretted it. I've been very fortunate since I came to this country. I've spent the greater part of my life in America.

Bill MacDonald had a more difficult time than most in becoming a citizen.

I got drafted in the service after three years here. And I imagine I put an extra effort into being a good soldier because I was an immigrant, and I felt I had to do at least as good as anybody here. All through my time in the service, I was repeatedly called in to the orderly room to be asked if I was still interested in becoming a citizen. And each time I said, "Of course." Then, that was it: "You're dismissed." It seemed like they were just thinking, let's give him the business, see how much he can take, and prove to us that he could be a good American citizen.

After having served the United States in the war in Korea, Bill returned to find he was still denied the better jobs because he was an alien.

When I came back to the States, I tried to get a job. The few places I went to . . . they had objections to the fact that I wasn't a citizen. Eventually I got a job for $1.25 an hour, and I had to be a master mechanic for this. They really exploited you. They knew you wouldn't dare quit. You had to do anything they told you to do. If you didn't have any mechanical work at some time, they made you cut the grass or clean the bathroom. It was really a sweatshop.

Finally, Bill MacDonald went to the courthouse in the New Jersey county where he lived and applied for citizenship.

I distinctly remember walking into the Union County Courthouse. I saw a bunch of people studying a little book. I didn't know what they were doing. Most of them couldn't speak English. They were older people, obviously here for years and years, and they were studying this book. I never received a book.

So this clerk started to ask individuals questions. They had their sponsor with them who would translate what the judge said, and refer maybe to a particular paragraph in the book, and they automatically write it out. And I'm listening to this, and thinking, this is what makes you a good citizen? This is crazy!

Well, the clerk came to me and he asked me something. I didn't have any book. It was something about some Indian chief. I never heard of the guy and I told him that I never heard of him. Then he went to task on me. He really ripped me apart. I was so embarrassed— no, not embarrassed—just plain mad. I could see myself digging my fingers into this guy's neck. Eventually I blew up and said, "If I wasn't an American citizen before I walked up those steps, I'm not going to be one when I walk back down. I think I earned my citizenship. I think I'm entitled to it."

It was a terrible system. It was really awful that, if you could answer the questions in this book, automatically you were a citizen. This is an awful way to measure loyalty. Luckily, the judge realized. He said, "Why do you say you earned your citizenship?" So I told him I just came out of the service. He was amazed. He didn't believe that I was in the service of the United States, in the army, and that I wasn't entitled automatically to citizenship. He said, "I never heard of that!" So that's how I got my citizenship.

Ian Keown explained why he had not yet become a citizen.

I've never actually decided that I'm not going back. I can't see myself as an American. I'm always going to be British. I think British, I act British, and I like being British, in fact. Although I've been living here for 18 years, I'm actually rather patriotic about Britain.

Some people get kind of miffed at this attitude. Because here you are—enjoying all the advantages of America, but you don't want to be an American. You don't want to take your responsibilities, and so forth. The only responsibility I don't take by adopting this attitude is that I don't vote. But I do pay taxes here. You perform all the obligations except voting—which is either an obligation or a privilege, depending on how you look at it. I'm getting a little more responsible about these things, and beginning to think I should be voting. But you can make your presence felt in other ways. You can write letters to government departments, and I'm constantly doing that.

Irish immigrants, in particular, have maintained an interest and involvement with politics in the home country even after becoming naturalized in the United States. IRA veteran Sean Lyons told about his activities.

All my spare time was spent, still is, on the Irish question. We collect money and send it back to help the revolutionary movement in Ireland, and to feed the wives and children of the men involved in it. Irish history repeats itself. In one generation you lose the fight, but you know that the next generation is going to pick up the fight and continue it. So when you become disabled, or outside the fight because you emigrate, well, you're going to help the new generation build up a revolution in any way you can.

Irish immigrants have been criticized for prolonging the violence in Ireland by supporting the revolutionary cause. No doubt this is true. The money they send goes to buy arms as well as food. But their experiences in Ireland have made many believe in the justice of this cause. The target of IRA activity today is Ulster. Maureen O'Donnell recalled some of the indignities and cruelties she experienced growing up a Catholic in Ulster:

We could not sing our national anthem. Not even at a gathering at home. One cannot sing the Irish national anthem in Northern Ireland. One must sing the British national anthem. People have served six and eight year jail sentences for singing patriot songs.

In my early years, there was a border campaign on, and through those long days and nights, for four years, there were British soldiers in Ireland as there are today. This was the '56 campaign. Our houses were ripped apart. A search of one's house could involve up to 40 or 50 British soldiers invading through windows, through doors, stairways, attics, basements, wherever they can enter. . . . You have no right to question why they are there.

Maureen O'Donnell remains devoted to the Catholic cause in Northern Ireland because she feels that it was injustice that forced her to leave and that injustice is draining Ireland of many of the young people who could help build up the nation.

It's one thing to really want to leave and explore the world, and another thing to be forced out of your home. One of the greatest exports of Ireland is her people, her sons and daughters. I would be very happy to be doing a day's work in Ireland and contributing to the land which I call home. I had to leave home. And while I like working in America and having made my home here, I don't advocate it for children of the future. I will do everything in my power to bring about a situation in Ireland that will create jobs for people in their own country.

Sean Lyons described his dual allegiances, to the United States and to Ireland, in a way that must sound familiar for most immigrants.

Of course, I'm an American. And at the same time I'm Irish, and this is something I can never deny—my birthright. Now the way I face it is, you love your mother. Yet get married. You love your wife. Does that mean you do not any longer love your mother? Not at all. They are two entirely different things. So I'm a citizen of America. I love the country, I respect all its laws. And at the same time I can't get away from the fact that I was born an Irishman. And the fact is that I would not have come to America if I could have lived in my own country, in any sort of capacity at all tolerable.

Notes

Asterisks (*) note that the spelling and punctuation of the quoted document have been modernized for the sake of clarity.

Chapter 1.   The First Ventures
1.* Quoted in Samuel Eliot Morison, *The European Discovery of America* (New York: Oxford University Press, 1971).
2.* Ibid.
3.* Quoted in Oscar T. Barck and Hugh T. Lefler, *Colonial America,* 2nd ed. (New York: Macmillan Co., 1968).
4.* Richard Hakluyt, *A Discourse Concerning Western Planting* (1584; Cambridge, Mass., 1877).
5.* Quoted in Robert Beverley, *The History and Present State of Virginia* (London, 1705).

Chapter 2.   The People of the British Isles
1. Quoted in R.L. Mackie, *A Short History of Scotland* (New York: Frederick A. Praeger, Publishers, 1963).

2. James Stephens, *Collected Poems,* (New York: Macmillan Co., 1926).

Chapter 3. "Planting" the New World

1.* George Chapman, Ben Jonson, and John Marston, *Eastward Hoe!* (London, 1605).
2.* Edward Arber, ed., *The Travels and Works of Captain John Smith* (Edinburgh: J. Grant, 1910).
3.* Thomas Morton, *New English Canaan* (Amsterdam, 1637).
4.* Beverley, *The History and Present State of Virginia.*
5.* H.R. McIlwaine, ed., *Journals of the House of Burgesses of Virginia* (Richmond, 1915).
6.* William Bradford, *Bradford's History "Of Plymouth Plantation," from the Original Manuscript* (Boston: 1898).
7.* Edward Winslow, *Mourt's Relation* (London, 1622).
8.* Bradford, *Of Plymouth Plantation.*
9.* John Hammond, *Leah and Rachel, or the Two Fruitfull Sisters, Virginia and Maryland* (London, 1656).
10.* Merrill Jensen, ed., *English Historical Documents: American Colonial Documents to 1776,* Vol. 9 (New York: Oxford University Press, 1955).
11. Quoted in John Commons, ed., *Documentary History of American Labor,* Vol. 1 (New York: American Heritage Publishing Co., 1971).
12. *The Virginia Gazette* (March 26, 1767).

Chapter 4. Not Only the English Come

1.* Quoted in Bernard Weisberger, *The American Heritage History of the American People.* (New York: American Heritage Publishing Co., 1971).

2.* Ibid.
3.* Quoted in Henry J. Ford, *The Scotch-Irish in America* (Princeton, N.J.: Princeton University Press, 1915).
4. Jonathan Swift, *Irish Tracts,* quoted in Curtis Nettels, *The Roots of American Civilization* (New York: F.S. Crofts, 1938).
5.* Hugh Boulter, *Letters Written by His Excellency Hugh Boulter* . . . (Dublin, 1770).
6.* Quoted in Charles A. Hanna, *The Scotch-Irish; or, The Scot in North Britain, North Ireland, and North America* (New York: G.P. Putnam's Sons, 1902).
7.* Quoted in Ford, *Scotch-Irish in America.*
8.* Jensen, *English Historical Documents.*
9.* Alexander Hamilton, *Gentleman's Progress: The Itinerarium of Dr. Alexander Hamilton, 1744,* ed. Carl Bridenbaugh (Chapel Hill,: University of North Carolina Press, 1948).
10.* Benjamin Franklin, *Information to Those Who Would Remove to America,* in Jared Sparks, ed., *The Works of Benjamin Franklin,* Vol. 2 (Chicago: 1882).

Chapter 5.   The English Colonies Become the American Nation
1.* Quoted in Sparks, *Works of Benjamin Franklin,* Vol. 4.
2.* Thomas Paine, *Common Sense* (Philadelphia, 1776).
3. John Adams, "The Meaning of the American Revolution," *Niles Weekly Register* (March 7, 1818).
4. "A Whig," *Pennsylvania Packet* (August 5, 1779).

5. Quoted in Max Farrand, ed., *The Records of the Federal Convention of 1787* (New Haven: Yale University Press, 1911).

Chapter 6. British and American Cousins

1. Charles Dickens, *Hard Times* (London, 1854).
2.* Rebecca Burlend, *A True Picture of Emigration: or, Fourteen Years in the Interior of North America,* ed. Milo M. Quaife (Chicago: Lakeside Press, 1936).
3. Quoted in J. Knight, ed., *Important Extracts from Original and Recent Letters Written by Englishmen in the United States of America to their Friends in England,* 2nd series (Manchester, 1818).
4.* Charlotte Erickson, *Invisible Immigrants: The Adaptation of English and Scottish Immigrants in Nineteenth-Century America.* (Coral Gables, Fla.: University of Miami Press, 1972).
5.* Knight, *Important Extracts from Original and Recent Letters.*

Chapter 7. Crossing the Atlantic and Getting Settled

1. Quoted in Edwin C. Guillet, *The Great Migration: The Atlantic Crossing by Sailing-ship Since 1770* (New York: Thomas Nelson, 1937).
2. Testimony of Samuel Sidney in *First Report from the Select Committee on Emigrant Ships* (House of Commons, 1854, Vol. 13).
3. William Chambers, "America Jottings, Emigrant Trappers," *Chamber's Edinburgh Journal* (March 3, 1855).

4.* Letter from Vere Foster in *Correspondence on the Treatment of the Passengers on Board the Emigrant Ship "Washington"* (House of Commons, 1851, Vol. 40).

5.* Quoted in Terry Coleman, *Going to America: A History of Emigrants from Great Britain and Ireland to America in the Mid-Nineteenth Century.* (New York: Pantheon, 1972).

6. Foster, *Treatment of Passengers on Board the "Washington."*

7. Quoted in Guillet, *The Great Migration.*

8. Quoted in Coleman, *Going to America.*

9. Ibid.

10.* Quoted in Guillet, *The Great Migration.*

11. Quoted in Alan Conway, ed., *The Welsh in America: Letters from the Immigrants.* (Minneapolis: University of Minnesota Press, 1961).

12. Quoted in Guillet, *The Great Migration.*

13. John Francis Maguire, *The Irish in America.* (New York: 1868).

14. Morris Birkbeck, *Letters from Illinois* (Philadelphia: 1818).

15. William Faux, *Memorable Days in America . . .* (London, 1823).

16. Conway, *The Welsh in America.*

17. Quoted in Erickson, *Invisible Immigrants.*

18. Ibid.

19. Quoted in Maldwyn A. Jones, *Destination America.* (New York: Holt, Rinehart and Winston, 1976).

20. Conway, *The Welsh in America.*

Chapter 8.   Ireland: The Famine Years

1. Quoted in Cecil Woodham-Smith, *The Great Hunger* (New York: Harper & Row, 1962).

2. *Gardener's Chronicle & Horticultural Gazette* (London, September 13, 1845).
3. Quoted in Charles Gavan Duffy, *Four Years of Irish History, 1845–1849* (New York, 1882).
4. Quoted in Woodham-Smith, *The Great Hunger.*
5. *The Times* (London, December 24, 1846).

Chapter 9. **"No Irish Need Apply"**
1. Quoted in *Journal of the American Irish Historical Society,* Vol. 12 (1912).
2. Quoted in Edith Abbott, *Historical Aspects of the Immigration Problem* (1926; reprint ed., New York: Arno Press, 1969).
3. Isabel Skelton, *The Life of Thomas D'Arcy McGee* (Gardenvale, Que.: Garden City Press, 1925).
4. Quoted in Carl Wittke, *The Irish in America.* (Baton Rouge: Louisiana State University Press, 1956).
5. Quoted in George W. Potter, *To the Golden Door.* (Boston: Little, Brown, 1960).
6. Quoted in William V. Shannon, *The American Irish.* (New York: Collier Books, 1974).
7. Quoted in *The Annals of America,* Vol. 7 (Chicago: Encyclopaedia Britannica, 1968).
8. Quoted in Arnold Schrier, *Ireland and the American Emigration, 1850–1900* (Minneapolis: University of Minnesota Press, 1958).
9. Quoted in Jones, *Destination America.*
10. Quoted in Barbara Kaye Greenleaf, *America Fever.* (New York: Four Winds Press, 1970).
11. *New York Evening Post* (September 4, 1830).
12. Quoted in *The Annals of America,* Vol. 7.
13. Quoted in Hamilton Holt, ed., *The Life Stories of Undistinguished Americans as Told by Themselves* (New York: James Pott & Co., 1906).

14. Quoted in Maguire, *The Irish in America.*
15. Quoted in Abbott, *Historical Aspects of the Immigration Problem.*
16. Quoted in Maguire, *The Irish in America.*
17. Quoted in Isaac A. Hourwich, *Immigration and Labor* (New York: G.P. Putnam's Sons, 1912).
18. Quoted in Maguire, *The Irish in America.*
19. Ibid.
20. Ibid.
21. John H. Griscom, *The Sanitary Conditions of the Laboring Population of New York . . .* , quoted in *The Annals of America,* Vol. 7.

Chapter 10.   America for Americans

1. Allan Nevins, ed., *The Diary of Philip Hone, 1828–1851* (New York: Dodd, Mead & Co., 1936).
2. Allan Nevins and Milton Halsey Thomas, eds., *The Diary of George Templeton Strong* (New York: Macmillan Co., 1952).
3. *Niles [Ohio] Weekly Register* (July 16, 1831).
4.* Quoted in John Tracy Ellis, ed., *Documents of American Catholic History* (Chicago: H. Regnery, 1967).
5. Samuel F.B. Morse, *Imminent Dangers to the Free Institutions of the United States through Foreign Immigration* (1835; reprint ed., New York: Arno Press, 1969).
6. Quoted in Stanley Feldstein and Lawrence Costello, eds., *The Ordeal of Assimilation: A Documentary History of the White Working Class* (Garden City, N.Y.: Doubleday, Anchor Press, 1974).
7. Quoted in Maguire, *The Irish in America.*
8. Quoted in Weisberger, *American Heritage History.*
9. Quoted in Arthur M. Schlesinger, Jr., *The Age of*

Jackson (Boston: Little, Brown & Company, 1945).
10. Quoted in Erickson, *Invisible Immigrants.*
11. J.T. Headley. *Pen and Pencil Sketches of the Great Riots . . .* (New York, 1882).

Chapter 11.   Leaders of Labor
1. Quoted in Clifton K. Yearley, Jr., *Britons in American Labor* (Westport, Ct: Greenwood Press, 1974).
2. Mary Harris Jones, *Autobiography of Mother Jones* (Chicago: C.H. Kerr, 1925).
3. Commons, *Documentary History of American Labor.*
4. Terence Powderly, *The Path I Trod: Autobiography of Terence Powderly,* eds. Harry J. Carman and Henry David (New York: Columbia University Press, 1940).
5. Jones, *Autobiography of Mother Jones.*

Chapter 12.   The Taking of Tammany and Other Irish Adventures in American Politics
1. *Boston Evening Transcript* (March 5, 1880), quoted in Weisberger, *American Heritage History.*
2. Quoted in William D. Griffin, ed., *The Irish in America.* (Dobbs Ferry, N.Y.: Oceana Publications, 1973).
3. Robert A. Woods, ed., *The City Wilderness: A Settlement Study . . .* (Boston: 1899).
4. Ibid.
5. E.L. Godkin, *The Nation* (October 18, 1966).
6. William L. Riordan, ed., *Plunkitt of Tammany Hall* (New York: McClure, Phillips, 1905).
7. Quoted in *The Annals of America,* Vol. 14.
8. *The New York Times* (September 13, 1960).

Chapter 13. **The Road Goes Ever On: Conversations with Irish and Scottish Immigrants**
All quotations in this chapter are based on interviews conducted by Visual Education Corporation. The interviews with Bill MacDonald, Maureen O'Donnell, Sean Lyons, and Jim O'Neill appear in *They Chose America* (Princeton, N.J.: Visual Education Corp., 1975). The interviews with John Darroch, Mary Darroch, and Ian Keown, conducted in 1979, have not previously been published.

Bibliography

Broehl, Wayne G., Jr. *The Molly Maguires.* Cambridge, Mass.: Harvard University Press, 1964.

Coleman, Terry. *Going to America.* New York: Pantheon Books, 1972.

Conway, Alan, ed. *The Welsh in America: Letters from the Immigrants.* Minneapolis: University of Minnesota Press, 1961.

Dickson, R. *Ulster Emigration to Colonial America, 1718–1775.* London: Routledge & Kegan Paul, 1966.

Erickson, Charlotte. *Invisible Immigrants: The Adaptation of English and Scottish Immigrants in Nineteenth-Century America.* Coral Gables, Fla.: University of Miami Press, 1972.

Furer, Howard B. *The British in America, 1578–1970.* Dobbs Ferry, N.Y.: Oceana Publications, 1972.

Greenleaf, Barbara Kaye. *America Fever.* New York: Four Winds Press, 1970.

Griffin, William D., ed. *The Irish in America.* Dobbs Ferry, N.Y.: Oceana Publications, 1973.

Handlin, Oscar. *Boston's Immigrants, 1790–1865.* Cambridge, Mass.: Harvard University Press, 1941.

Hartmann, Edward George. *Americans from Wales.* Boston: Christopher Publishing House, 1967.

Higham, John. *Strangers in the Land: Patterns of American Nativism 1860–1925.* New Brunswick, N.J.: Rutgers University Press, 1955.

Jones, Maldwyn A. *Destination America.* New York: Holt, Rinehart & Winston, 1976.

Leyburn, James Graham. *The Scotch-Irish: A Social History.* Chapel Hill: University of North Carolina Press, 1962.

Maguire, John Francis. *The Irish in America.* 1868. Reprint. New York: Arno Press, 1969.

Morison, Samuel Eliot. *The European Discovery of America.* New York: Oxford University Press, 1971.

O'Grady, Joseph P. *How the Irish Became Americans.* New York: Twayne Publishers, 1973.

Potter, George W. *To the Golden Door.* Boston: Little, Brown & Company, 1960.

Rowe, John. *The Hard Rock Men: Cornish Immigrants and the North American Mining Frontier.* Liverpool: Liverpool University Press, 1974.

Seller, Maxine. *To Seek America.* Englewood, N.J.: Jerome S. Ozer, 1977.

Shannon, William V. *The American Irish.* New York: Collier Books, 1974.

Wakin, Edward. *Enter the Irish-Americans.* New York: Thomas Y. Crowell Co., 1976.

Weisberger, Bernard. *The American Heritage History of the American People.* New York: American Heritage Publishing Co., 1971.

Wittke, Carl. *The Irish in America.* Baton Rouge: Louisiana State University Press, 1956.

Woodham-Smith, Cecil. *The Great Hunger.* New York: Harper & Row, Publishers, 1962.

Wright, Louis Booker, ed. *The Elizabethans' America: A Collection of Early Reports by Englishmen on the New World.* Cambridge, Mass.: Harvard University Press, 1965.

Yearley, Clifton K., Jr. *Britons in American Labor.* Westport, Conn.: Greenwood Press, 1974.

A Brief History of U.S. Immigration Laws

The authority to formulate immigration policy rests with Congress and is contained in Article 1, Section 8, Clause 3 of the Constitution, which provides that Congress shall have the power to "regulate commerce with foreign nations, and among the several States, and with the Indian tribes."

Alien Act of 1798: authorized the deportation of aliens by the President. Expired after two years.

For the next seventy-five years there was no federal legislation restricting admission to, or allowing deportation from, the United States.

Act of 1875: excluded criminals and prostitutes and entrusted inspection of immigrants to collectors of the ports.

Act of 1882: excluded lunatics and idiots and persons liable to becoming a public charge.

First Chinese Exclusion Act.

Acts of 1885 and 1887: contract labor laws, which made it unlawful to import aliens under contract for labor or services of any kind. (Exceptions: artists, lecturers, servants, skilled aliens in an industry not yet established in the United States, etc.)

178

Act of 1888: amended previous acts to provide for expulsion of aliens landing in violation of contract laws.

Act of 1891: first exclusion of persons with certain diseases; felons, also persons having committed crimes involving moral turpitude; polygamists, etc.

Act of 1903: further exclusion of persons with certain mental diseases, epilepsy, etc; beggars; also "anarchists or persons who believe in, or advocate the overthrow by force or violence of the Government of the United States or of all government or of all forms of law or the assassination of public officials." Further refined deportation laws.

Acts of 1907, 1908: further exclusions for health reasons, such as TB.

Exclusion of persons detrimental to labor conditions in the United States, specifically Japanese and Korean skilled or unskilled laborers.

Gentlemen's Agreement with Japan: in which Japan agreed to restrictions imposed by the United States.

Act of 1917: codified previous exclusion provisions, and added literacy test. Further restricted entry of other Asians.

Act of 1921: First Quota Law, in which approximately 350,000 immigrants were permitted entry, mostly from northern or western Europe.

Act of 1924: National Origins Quota System set annual limitations on the number of aliens of any nationality immigrating to the U.S. The act also decreed, in a provision aimed primarily at the Japanese, that no alien ineligible for citizenship could be admitted to the U.S.

"Gigolo Act" of 1937: allowing deportation of aliens fraudulently marrying in order to enter the United States either by having marriage annulled or by refusing to marry once having entered the country.

Act of 1940: Alien Registration Act provided for registration and fingerprinting of all aliens.

Act of 1943: Chinese Exclusion Acts repealed.

Act of 1945: War Brides Act admitted during the three years of act's existence approximately 118,000 brides, grooms, and children of servicemen who had married foreign nationals during World War II.

Act of 1949: Displaced Persons Act admitted more than four hundred thousand people displaced as a result of World War II (to 1952).

Act of 1950: Internal Security Act excluded from immigrating any present of foreign member of the Communist party, and made more easily deportable people of this class already in the U.S. Also provided for alien registration by January 10 of each year.

Act of 1952: Immigration and Nationality Act codified all existing legislation; also eliminated race as a bar to immigration.

Acts of 1953–1956: Refugee Relief acts admitted orphans, Hungarians after 1956 uprising, skilled sheepherders.

1957: special legislation to admit Hungarian refugees.

1960: special legislation paroled Cuban refugees into the U.S.

Act of 1965: legislation amending act of 1952 phased out national origins quotas by 1968, with new numerical ceilings on a first come, first served basis. Numerical ceilings (per annum): 120,000 for natives of the Western Hemisphere; 170,000 for natives of the Eastern Hemisphere. New preference categories: relatives (74 percent), scientists, artists (10 percent), skilled and unskilled labor (10 percent), refugees (6 percent).

Act of 1977: allowed Indo-Chinese who had been paroled into the U.S. to adjust their status to permanent resident.

1979: Presidential directive allowed thousands of Vietnamese "boat people" to enter the U.S.

Index